Hands-On Math

Learning Addition and Subtraction through Manipulative Activities

By

Dr. Kathleen Fletcher-Bacer

Note for Librarians: a cataloguing record for this book that includes Dewey
Decimal Classification and US Library of Congress numbers is available from
the Library and Archives of Canada. The complete cataloguing record can be
obtained from their online database at:
www.collectionscanada.ca/amicus/index-e.html
ISBN 1-4120-4126-0
Printed in Victoria, BC, Canada

TRAFFORD

Offices in Canada, USA, Ireland, UK and Spain
This book was published on-demand in cooperation with Trafford Publishing.
On-demand publishing is a unique process and service of making a book
available for retail sale to the public taking advantage of on-demand
manufacturing and Internet marketing. On-demand publishing includes
promotions, retail sales, manufacturing, order fulfilment, accounting and
collecting royalties on behalf of the author.
Book sales for North America and international:
Trafford Publishing, 6E–2333 Government St.,
Victoria, BC v8t 4p4 CANADA
phone 250 383 6864 (toll-free 1 888 232 4444)
fax 250 383 6804; email to orders@trafford.com
Books sales in Europe:
Trafford Publishing (uk) Ltd., Enterprise House,
Wistaston Road Business Centre,
Wistaston Road, Crewe. Cheshire cw2 7rp UNITED KINGDOM
phone 01270 251 396 (local rate 0845 230 9601)
facsimile 01270 254 983; orders.uk@trafford.com
Order online at:
www.trafford.com/robots/04-1933.html

10 9 8 7 6

Table of Contents

ABOUT THIS BOOK

I hear and I forget.
I see and I remember.
I do and I understand.
Chinese Proverb

Hands-on Math is based on this proverb. The use of manipulatives is the key to enabling students to understand abstract mathematical concepts. With the National Council of Teachers of Mathematics' Standards (NCTM) serving as a model for what should be occurring in mathematics classrooms, manipulatives are now essential. Learning how to use manipulatives in the classroom, however, is challenging. If the manipulatives are not presented in the correct manner, they may serve to confuse the student rather than enhance learning.

It is very important to use manipulatives in the manner they are designed – to develop those very important foundational mathematical concepts throughout the grade levels, thus making mathematics understandable to children. It has been my experience that children who discover foundational mathematical concepts for themselves retain those concepts and are able to transfer them beautifully to higher levels of mathematics.

The purpose of this book is to provide the teacher with a realistic approach to teaching with manipulatives. Use the activities to teach and develop the foundational skill and then utilize the manipulatives right along with textbook and supportive materials.

Addition and subtraction operations is part of the NCTM "Number and Operations" standard. It encompasses understanding the meaning of addition and subtraction relationships and gaining computational fluency. This book is designed to assist the teacher in addressing this standard.

The book is divided into specific addition and subtraction skills categories. Each activity is organized under the specific skill it develops in the table of contents. When you are in need of a lesson plan or a math exercise for your students, simply choose one suited to the skill you are teaching.

The ✿ symbol identifies the teacher pages. Each of these pages outlines a manipulative lesson for you to follow. Quite often, a student page accompanies a teacher page so that the concept may be strengthened by student practice.

Each page, labeled with a ✏ symbol invites students to investigate a concept. These student pages are intended to be used initially with the teacher's direction. Once underway, however, the student pages may be completed by individual students with little teacher involvement.

Get ready for math to become a favorite subject!

Activities
for the
Basic Addition Facts

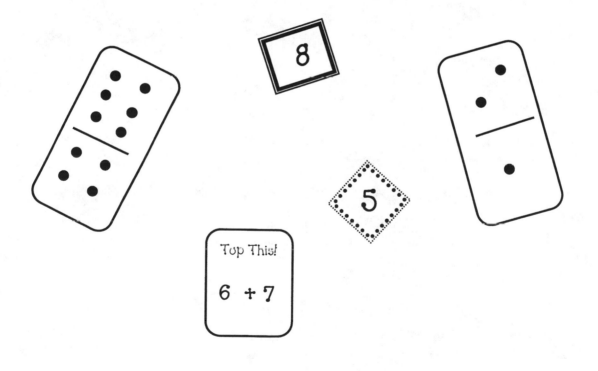

ADDITION CONCEPT:
Developing addition facts with sums to 10

Unifix it to 10

Preparation:
- Supply each student with three sets of ten unifix cubes – each set a different color.

- Distribute nine copies of the *Unifix it to 10* worksheet (page 4) to each student.

- Students will need crayons the same color as their unifix cubes.

Procedure:
- Ask the students to take one set of unifix cubes and form a bar as long as they want (e.g. 8 blue cubes).

- Before students begin the worksheet, make sure they record the number of cubes selected i.e., facts of **8**, at the top of their worksheet. Color the first row to match the chain they formed (8 blue squares).

- With the remaining two colors of unifix cubes, students will create as many different combinations as they can that equal the first chain. (e.g., 4 reds and 4 yellows).

- Students record each combination made by coloring in the grid on the worksheet and writing the corresponding number sentence.

- Activity continues with students repeating the procedure with the other facts for the numbers 1-10.   *Example:* ***facts of 8***

1	2	3	4	5	6	7	8	9	10	Addition Sentence
▓	▓	▓	▓	▓	▓	▓	▓			8+0=8
				▓	▓	▓	▓			4+4=8
▓	▓									2+6=8

Unifix it to 10

Facts of _____

1	2	3	4	5	6	7	8	9	10	Addition Sentence

Name_____ Date_____

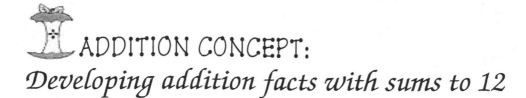

ADDITION CONCEPT:
Developing addition facts with sums to 12

Domino It

Preparation:
- Supply each student with a set of Double-Six dominoes. If commercially made dominoes are not available, use the Double-Six domino pattern on page 6. Copy the pattern on cardstock paper, cut out the sets and store in closeable bags. You may want to reproduce each set on a different color of cardstock or number the back of the domino sets to avoid the sets getting mixed up when the students are working with them.

- Each student will need a copy of the **Domino It!** worksheets on pages 7-9.

- Make an overhead transparency of the domino pattern and worksheets for illustration purposes. Cut out the Double-Six domino pattern to create dominoes for the overhead projector.

Procedure:
- Using the overhead dominoes and worksheets, demonstrate how students count and record with the dominoes. Each half of the domino is considered an addend in the addition problem.

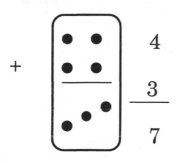

- Students use their dominoes to solve pages 7-8.
- As an extension activity, students can design problems for each other using the worksheet on page 9.

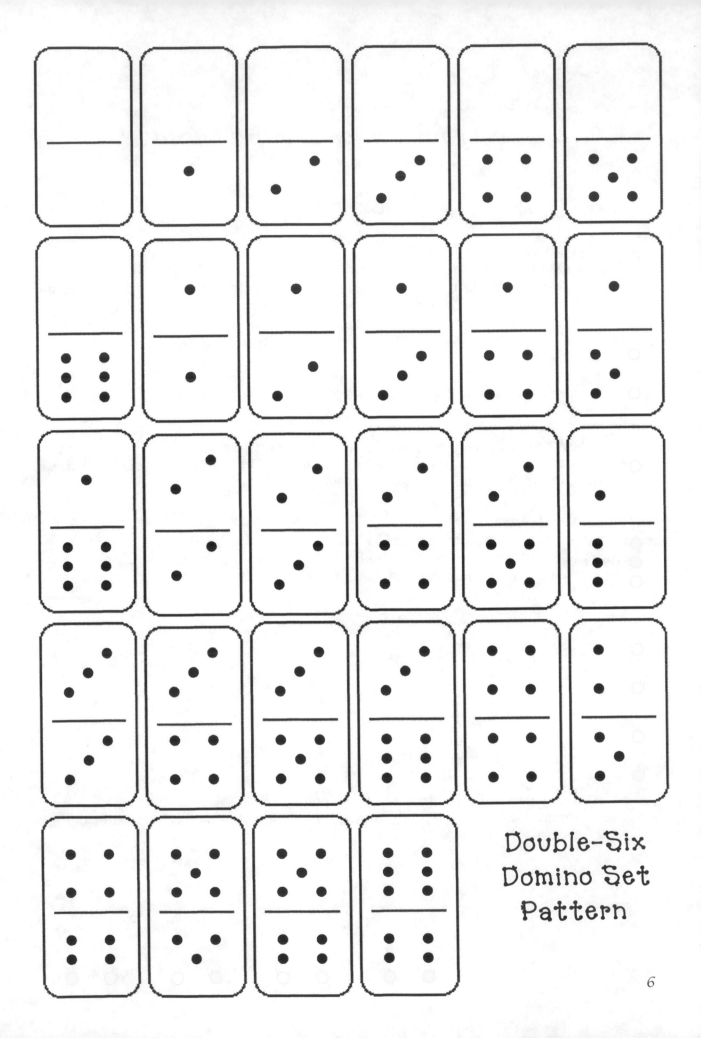

Double-Six
Domino Set
Pattern

6

Domino It!

Find the domino that solves each sum. Draw the missing dots. Don't use the same domino twice.

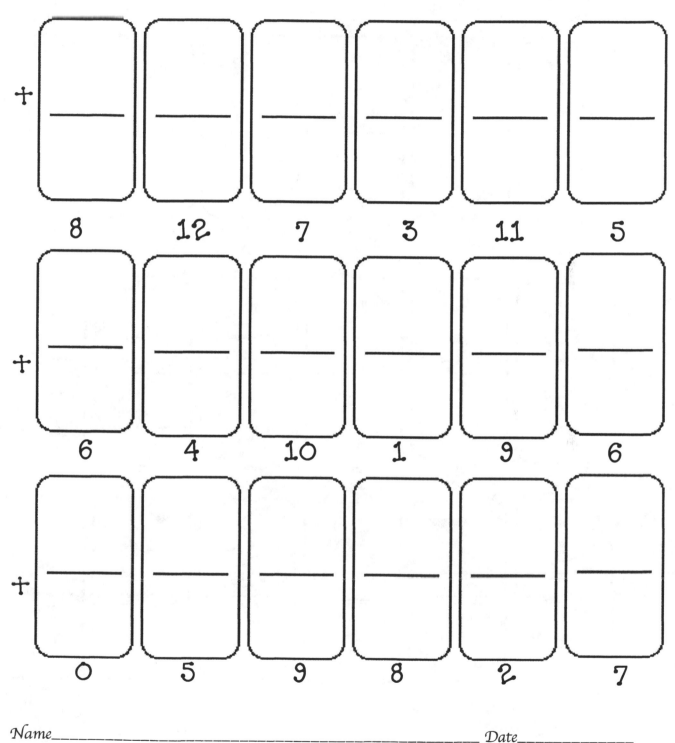

✝

8 12 7 3 11 5

✝

6 4 10 1 9 6

✝

0 5 9 8 2 7

Name_____ Date_____

Domino It!

Find the domino that solves each sum. Draw the missing dots. Don't use the same domino twice.

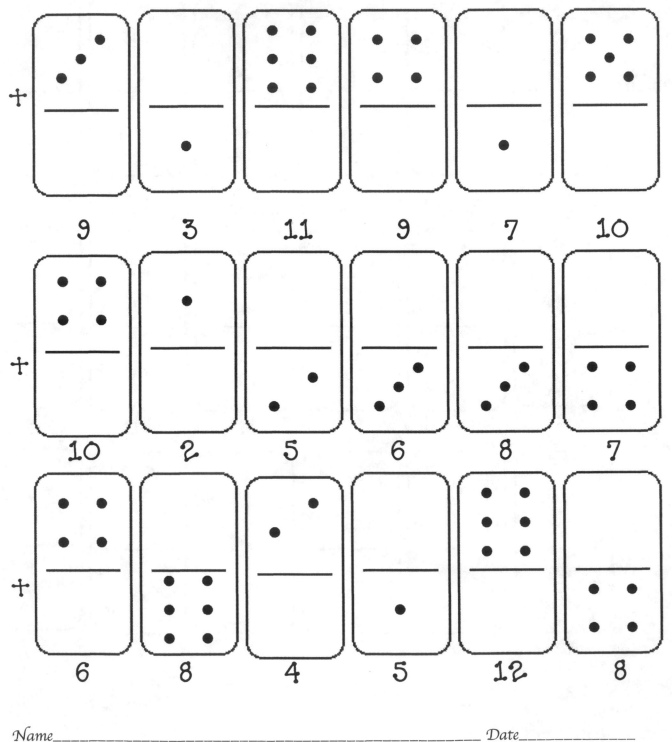

+   9   3   11   9   7   10

+   10   2   5   6   8   7

+   6   8   4   5   12   8

Name_____ Date_____

©2004 Bacer,K Hands-On Math: Learning +&- through Manipulative Activities   8

Domino It!

Make a *Domino It!* page for a friend. Draw dots for the top half of the domino and fill in the desired sum. Ask a friend to find the domino that solves each domino problem and draw in the correct number of dots. Don't use the same domino twice.

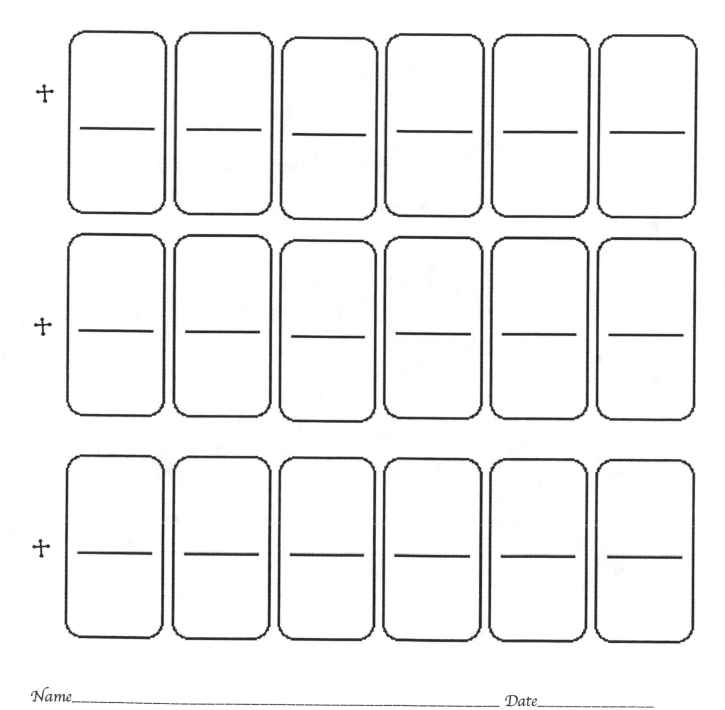

Name_____ Date_____

ADDITION CONCEPT:
Reinforcing basic addition facts with sums to 12

Domino Solitaire to 12

Preparation:
- Provide each pair of students with a set of Double-Six dominoes. If commercially made dominoes are not available, use the Double-Six domino pattern on page 6 and follow construction instructions from page 5.

Procedure:
- Each pair of students turn six dominoes face up in their playing area. One partner looks for any two dominoes that together have a total sum of twelve dots.

  Example:

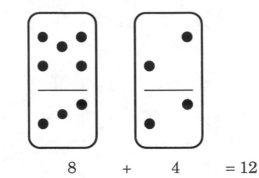

$$8 \quad + \quad 4 \quad = 12$$

- The two dominoes are set aside and two additional dominoes are turned face up.

- With partners alternating turns, play continues with the search for two dominoes equaling 12.

- Two new dominoes replace the two matched up each time.

- If the entire set of dominoes can be paired off in twelves, solitaire 12 has been cracked.

- If there comes a time in the game where no two dominoes equals 12, the game is lost – TRY AGAIN!

Variations of this game:

- Change the number of face-up dominoes to 8 or 10.

- Play the game in authentic solitaire tradition with only one player and a set of dominoes

Example :

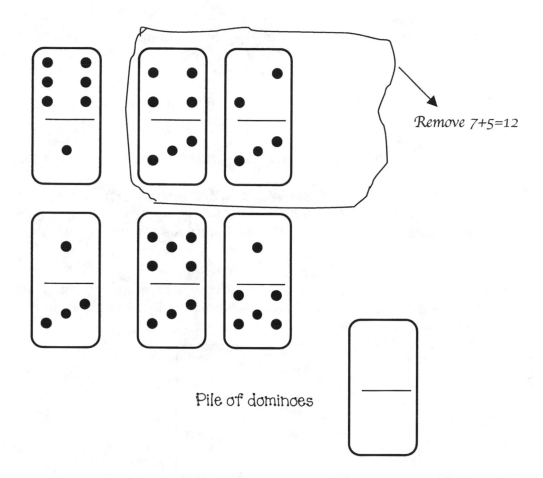

Remove 7+5=12

Pile of dominoes

ADDITION CONCEPT:
Developing addition facts with sums to 18

Domino Sum It

Preparation:

- Supply each student with a set of Double-Six dominoes. If commercially made dominoes are not available, use the Double-Six domino pattern on page 6 and follow construction instructions from page 5.

- Make an overhead transparency of the ***Domino Sum It!*** worksheets on pages 13-16.

- Each student will also need a copy of the ***Domino Sum It!*** worksheets.

- Make an overhead transparency of the domino pattern and worksheets for illustration purposes. Cut out the Double-Six domino pattern to create dominoes for the overhead projector. Overhead dominoes are also available commercially.

Procedure:

- Using the overhead dominoes and worksheet transparencies, illustrate how students will find the sum of two dominoes and record their answers on the worksheets.

    Example:

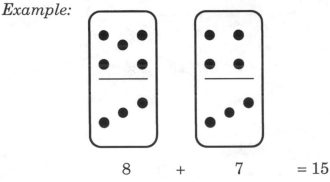

$$8 \quad + \quad 7 \quad = 15$$

- The worksheet on page 14 allows students to find the missing addend.

- Use the worksheet on page 16 for students to develop problems for their classmates to solve.

Domino Sum It

Fill in the lines with each domino sum.

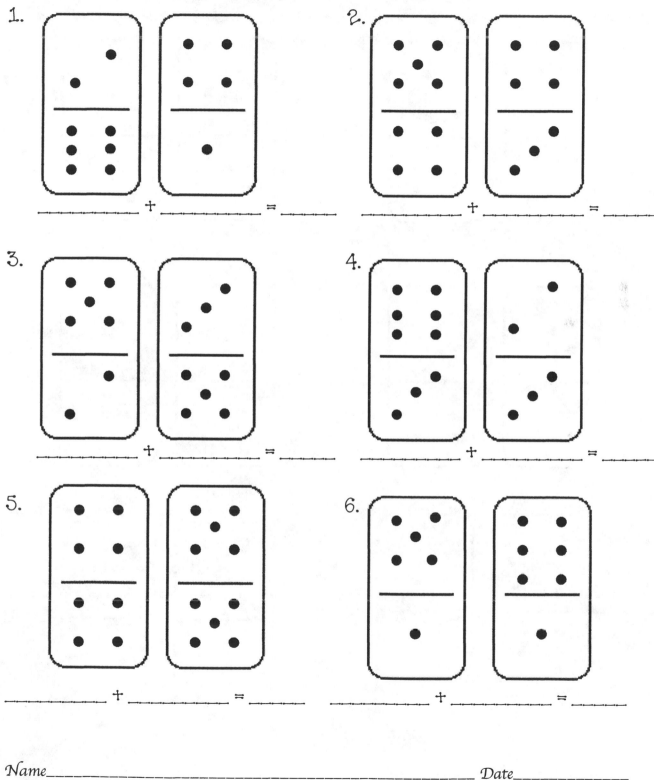

1.

_____ + _____ = _____

2.

_____ + _____ = _____

3.

_____ + _____ = _____

4.

_____ + _____ = _____

5.

_____ + _____ = _____

6.

_____ + _____ = _____

Name_____ Date_____

Domino Sum It

Find the domino that matches and solves the sum. Draw the missing dots and sums.

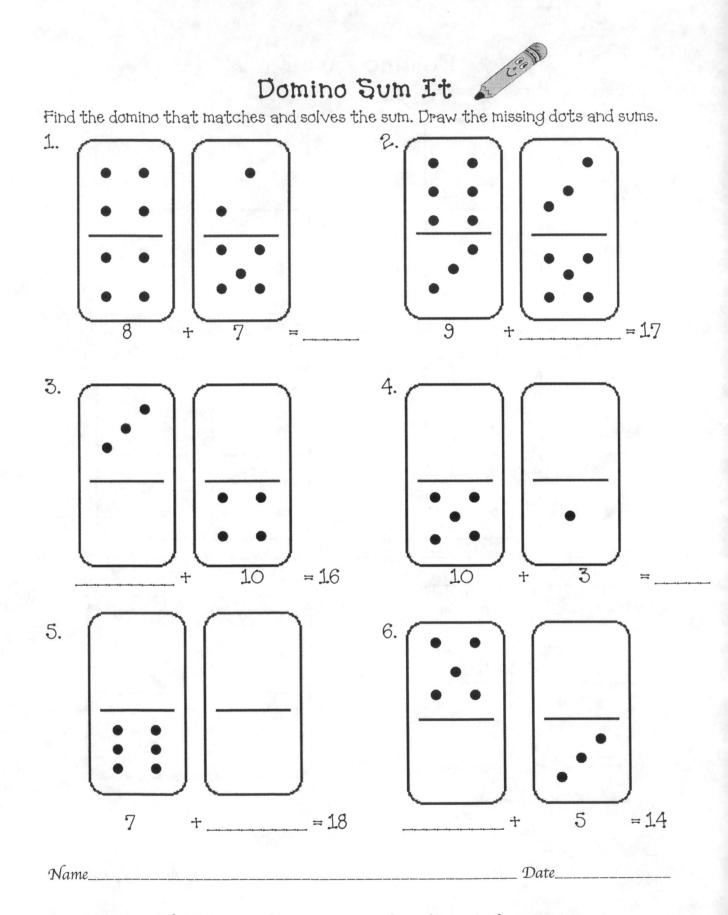

1. 8 + 7 = _____

2. 9 + _____ = 17

3. _____ + 10 = 16

4. 10 + 3 = _____

5. 7 + _____ = 18

6. _____ + 5 = 14

Name_____ Date_____

Domino Sum It

Find the domino that matches and solves the sum. Draw the missing dots and sums.

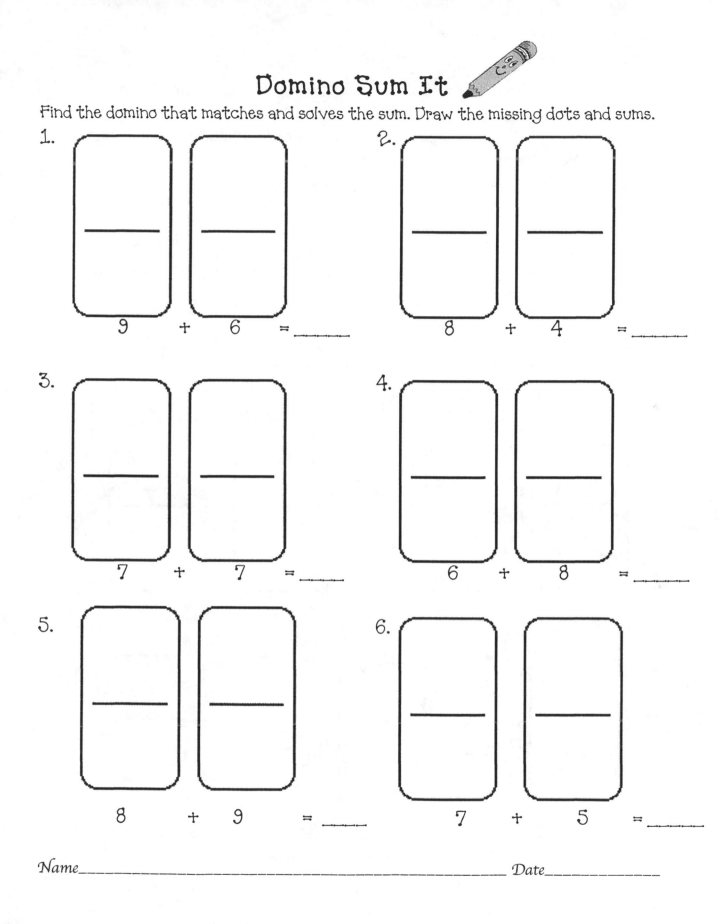

1.   9   +   6   = _____

2.   8   +   4   = _____

3.   7   +   7   = _____

4.   6   +   8   = _____

5.   8   +   9   = _____

6.   7   +   5   = _____

Name_____ Date_____

Domino Sum It

Make a *Domino It!* page for a friend. Draw dots for the top half or bottom half of the domino and fill in the desired sum. Ask a friend to find the domino that solves each domino problem and draw in the correct number of dots.

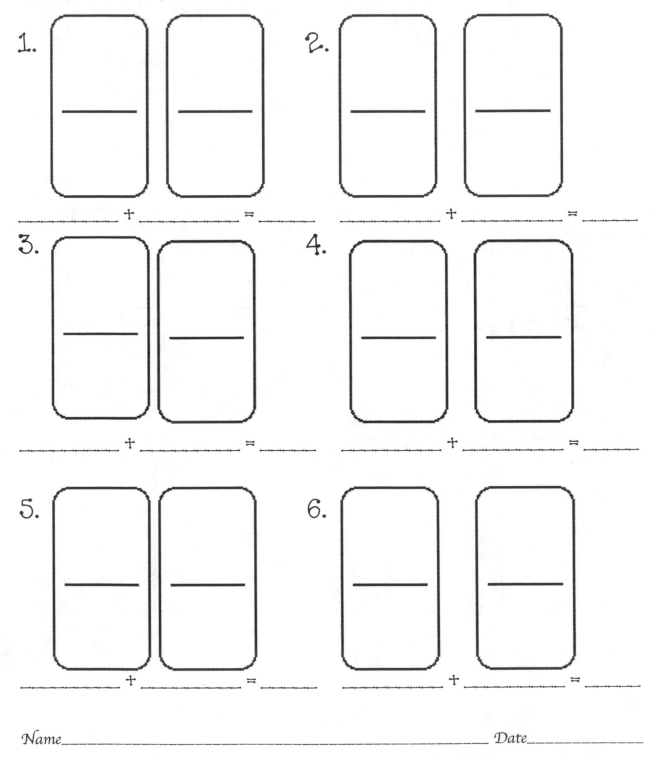

1. ____ + ____ = ____

2. ____ + ____ = ____

3. ____ + ____ = ____

4. ____ + ____ = ____

5. ____ + ____ = ____

6. ____ + ____ = ____

Name_____ Date_____

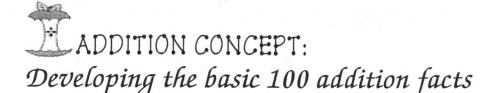

ADDITION CONCEPT:
Developing the basic 100 addition facts

Dice It

Preparation:
- A pair of standard dice can be used for set C, but all the other sets will have to be made by writing the various numbers with a permanent marker onto blank 1cm wooden cubes. Use a different color permanent marker for each set.

- Reproduce the **Dice It** recording sheet (page 17) so that each pair of students has a copy.

Set	Numerals	Set	Numerals
A	0,1,2,2,3,4	D	1,2,3,5,6,7
B	0,2,4,5,7,9	E	1,2,3,5,7,9
C	1,2,3,4,5,6	F	4,5,6,7,8,9

Procedure:
- Divide students into partners.

- Select two pair of dice according to needs/abilities for each set of partners

- Dice sets are listed in order of increasing difficult. Different combinations of dice can be used for additional games.

- The worksheet is completed by each partner rolling the pair of dice and recording the addend and the sum on their side of the worksheet.

- Partners can race against each other or take turns completing the worksheet. Points may be earned for correct answers.

Variations of this game:
Students can work individually completing both sides of the worksheet.

Dice It!

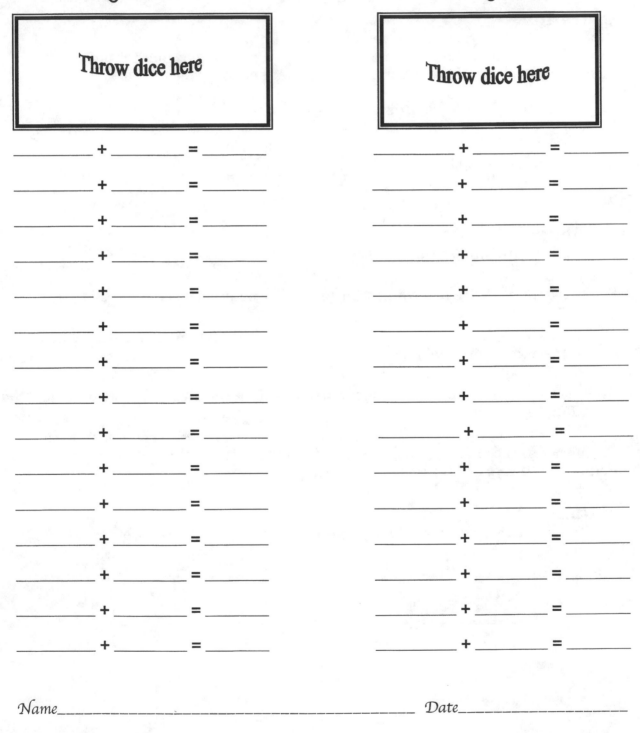

Player 1

Throw dice here

_____ + _____ = _____

_____ + _____ = _____

_____ + _____ = _____

_____ + _____ = _____

_____ + _____ = _____

_____ + _____ = _____

_____ + _____ = _____

_____ + _____ = _____

_____ + _____ = _____

_____ + _____ = _____

_____ + _____ = _____

_____ + _____ = _____

_____ + _____ = _____

_____ + _____ = _____

_____ + _____ = _____

Player 2

Throw dice here

_____ + _____ = _____

_____ + _____ = _____

_____ + _____ = _____

_____ + _____ = _____

_____ + _____ = _____

_____ + _____ = _____

_____ + _____ = _____

_____ + _____ = _____

_____ + _____ = _____

_____ + _____ = _____

_____ + _____ = _____

_____ + _____ = _____

_____ + _____ = _____

_____ + _____ = _____

_____ + _____ = _____

Name_____ Date_____

ADDITION CONCEPT:
Reinforcing the basic addition facts with the addition table

Mixed up Addition Facts

Preparation:
- One sheet of graph paper with one-centimeter squares for each student (use page 20)

- An overhead transparency of page 20.

- Overhead transparency markers to illustrate work.

Procedure:
- Using the overhead transparency, illustrate how to mark off a 10 by 10cm area in the middle of the graph paper.

- Students will randomly write any numeral 0-9 across the top and along the left-hand side.

- Solve the mixed up puzzle by adding the left-hand side number to the corresponding top number. The answer goes where the two numbers intersect.
  Example:

+	5	7	2	4	1	9	6	8	3	0
2	7	9	4	6	3	11	8	10	5	2
4										
7										
9										
0										
8										
3										
1										
5										
6										

One-Centimeter Graph Paper

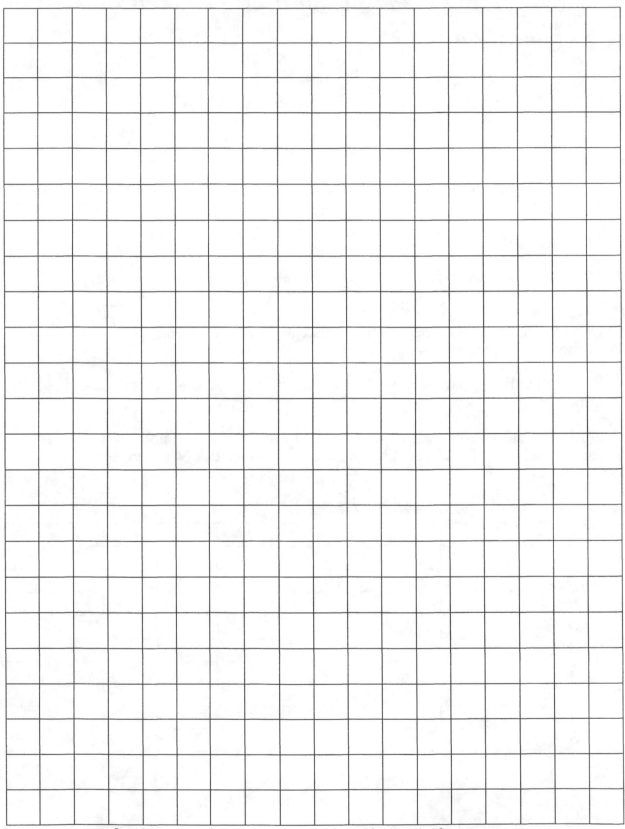

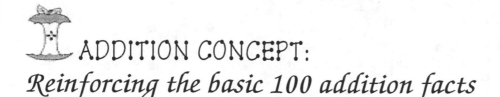 ADDITION CONCEPT:
Reinforcing the basic 100 addition facts

Domino War

Preparation:
*   Supply each pair of students with a set of Double-Nine set of dominoes. If commercially made dominoes are not available, duplicate the pattern on page 21 and 6 onto cardstock, cut apart and follow the assembly instructions on page 5.

Procedure:
*   Dominoes are placed face down in the center of the playing area.

*   Each player turns over a domino and says the entire addition sentence.

Example:

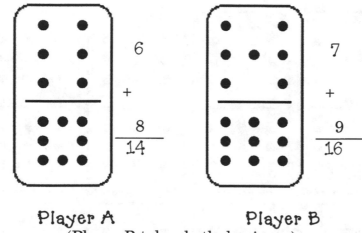

Player A   Player B
(Player B takes both dominoes)

*   The partner with the larger sum takes both dominoes and places them in their pile. If one of the partners makes an error and the other corrects them, then that partner gets both dominoes.

*   If a tie occurs "war" is declared and two more dominoes are turned over. The winner takes all four dominoes.

*   The game continues until all the dominoes have been compared. The player with the most dominoes wins.

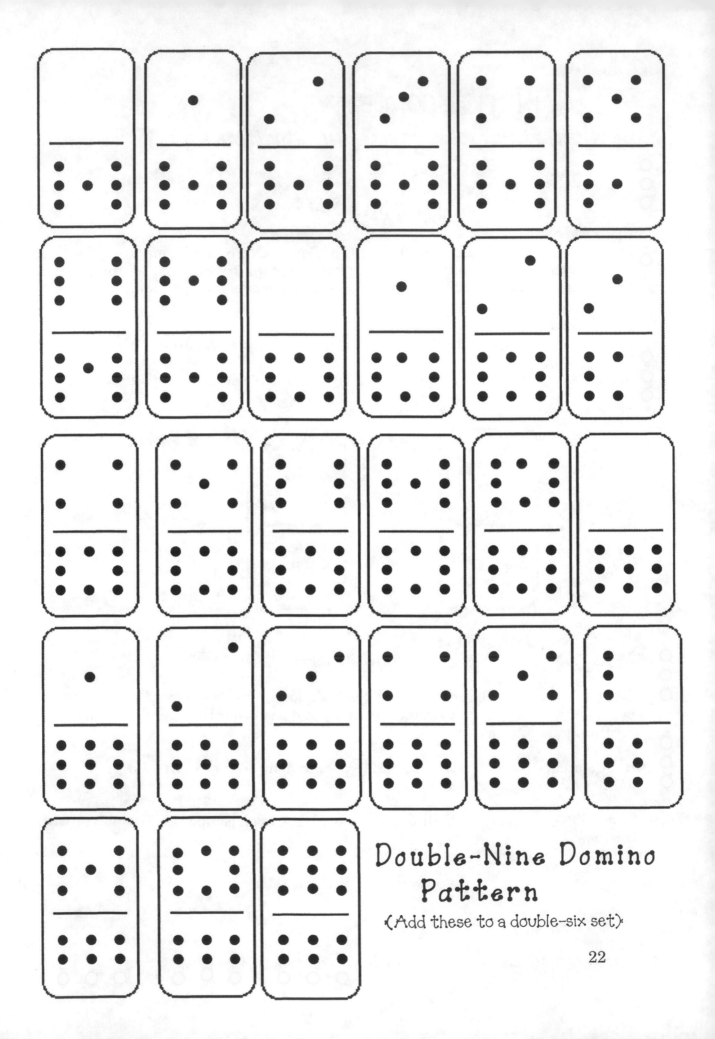

Double-Nine Domino Pattern

(Add these to a double-six set)

22

ADDITION CONCEPT:
Developing the basic 100 addition facts with two three addends

Undercover

Preparation:
- Reproduce the ***Under Cover*** gameboard (page 24) for each student.

- Provide transparent game markers for each students.

- Distribute 3 sets of regular dice to each pair of students.

Procedure:
- Divide students into groups of two.

- Players roll one die to determine who goes first.

- Each player must decide how many die/dice they want to roll before each turn (1,2,or 3).

- Each turn consists of throwing the selected amount of die/dice, finding the sum of the die/dice, and covering up one space that matches that sum on the game board.

- The first player to have a horizontal or vertical row "under cover" is the winner.

Variations of the game:
- If the board is covered before anyone wins, players can remove an opponents marker that is in the occupied space of the corresponding sum rolled.

- Play continues until the game board is "undercover". The player with the most markers wins.

- Create different gameboards and different sets of numbered dice.

Undercover

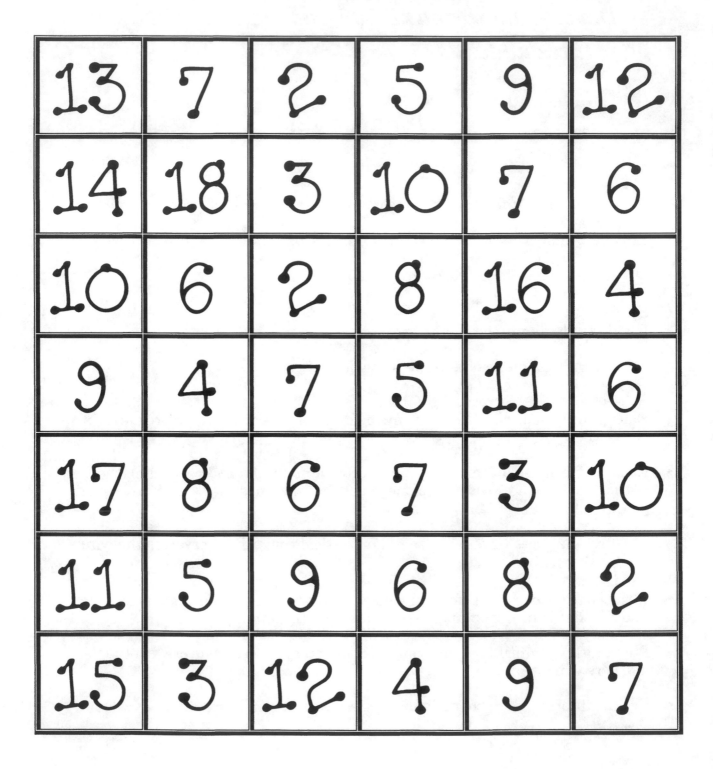

13	7	2	5	9	12
14	18	3	10	7	6
10	6	2	8	16	4
9	4	7	5	11	6
17	8	6	7	3	10
11	5	9	6	8	2
15	3	12	4	9	7

ADDITION CONCEPT:
Understanding basic addition facts using three Addends

Sum Speed

Preparation:
* Provide each student with blank paper and a pencil.

Procedure:
* Instruct students to draw the following diagram on their papers.

* Assign each student a sum between 12-18. Students will write that sum at the top of their paper.
* The grid is used to create three addends from left to right totaling the given sum.
* The same sequence cannot be repeated twice.
* Students may correct their neighbor's paper. Each error counts as a point. The object of the game is not to score points.

14 is the sum of this example

7	2	5
4	3	7
1	9	4
6	5	3
8	1	5
3	5	6

ADDITION CONCEPT:
Practicing the 100 basic addition facts

Top This

Preparation:
- Duplicate pages 27-32 onto cardstock. Cut out the set to make a deck of cards. Each group of 2, 4, or 6 students will need at least two complete decks.

Procedure:
- The shuffled deck is dealt evenly to each player in a group of 2,4,or 6 students.

- Placing the cards face down, each player turns over their top card.

- Player is to read the addition sentence aloud, i.e., for 7+5, seven plus five equals twelve – 1 ten and 2 ones. This builds an important thinking foundation for regrouping.

- The player's card with the highest sum takes all the top cards and places them in their own individual pile.

- If a tie occurs, each player involved turns over the next top card and the highest takes all the top cards.

- The player that ends up with the most cards in their individual pile is the winner.

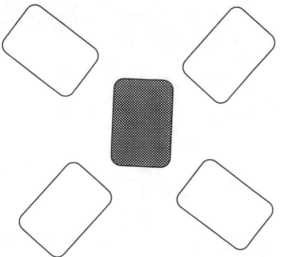

Top This Cards

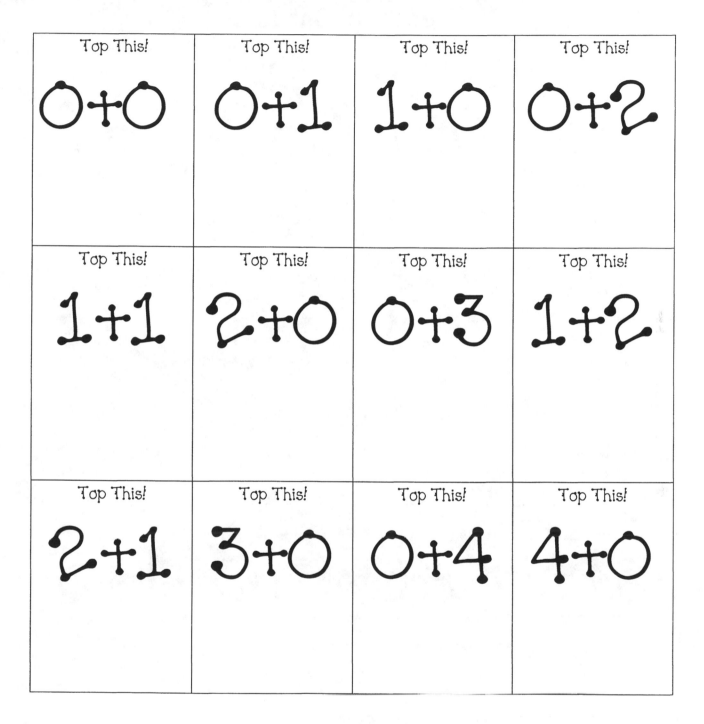

Top This!	Top This!	Top This!	Top This!
0+0	0+1	1+0	0+2

Top This!	Top This!	Top This!	Top This!
1+1	2+0	0+3	1+2

Top This!	Top This!	Top This!	Top This!
2+1	3+0	0+4	4+0

Top This Cards

Top This! 1+3	Top This! 3+1	Top This! 2+2	Top This! 0+5
Top This! 5+0	Top This! 1+4	Top This! 4+1	Top This! 2+3
Top This! 3+2	Top This! 0+6	Top This! 6+0	Top This! 1+5

Top This Cards

Top This!	Top This!	Top This!	Top This!
5+1	2+4	4+2	3+3
Top This!	Top This!	Top This!	Top This!
0+7	7+0	1+6	6+1
Top This!	Top This!	Top This!	Top This!
2+5	5+2	3+4	4+3

Top This Cards

Top This!	Top This!	Top This!	Top This!
0+8	8+0	1+7	7+1

Top This!	Top This!	Top This!	Top This!
2+6	6+2	3+5	5+3

Top This!	Top This!	Top This!	Top This!
4+4	0+9	9+0	1+8

Top This Cards

Top This!	Top This!	Top This!	Top This!
8+1	2+7	7+2	3+6
Top This!	Top This!	Top This!	Top This!
6+3	4+5	5+4	0+10
Top This!	Top This!	Top This!	Top This!
10+0	1+9	9+1	2+8

Top This Cards

Top This!	Top This!	Top This!	Top This!
$8+2$	$3+7$	$7+3$	$4+6$
Top This!	Top This!	Top This!	Top This!
$6+4$	$5+5$	$2+9$	$9+2$
Top This!	Top This!	Top This!	Top This!
$3+8$	$8+3$	$4+7$	$7+4$

Top This Cards

Top This!	Top This!	Top This!	Top This!
5+6	6+5	3+9	9+3

Top This!	Top This!	Top This!	Top This!
4+8	8+4	5+7	7+5

Top This!	Top This!	Top This!	Top This!
6+6	4+9	9+4	5+8

ACTIVITES
FOR THE
ADDITION PROPERTIES

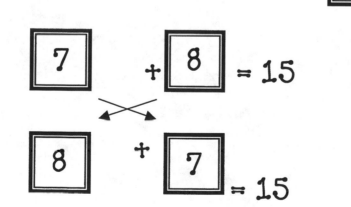

ADDITION CONCEPT:
Understanding the commutative property of Addition

Commutative & Dice

Preparation:
*   Duplicate the ***Commutative Property of Addition*** worksheet on page 38 for each student.

*   Provide each student with dice sets D and F from page 17.

*   Copy page 38 onto an overhead transparency for demonstration purposes.

*   Make an overhead die by cutting squares of acetate and writing die numerals with an overhead marker.

Background Information:
The commutative property of addition states that for any whole number a and b, a+b=b+a. In other words, no matter what order you add the same two numbers together, the sum will always be the same.

Procedure:
*   As each die is rolled, it is placed in the **die** square on the worksheet. The dice represent the addends that will generate the sum.

*   Slide the dice along the arrows and record the addends and sum again.

*   Complete the worksheet by repeating the process.

*   Encourage students to verbalize the pattern they see and then write the rule and pattern.

$$5 + 4 = 9$$
$$4 + 5 = 9$$

Commutative Property of Addition

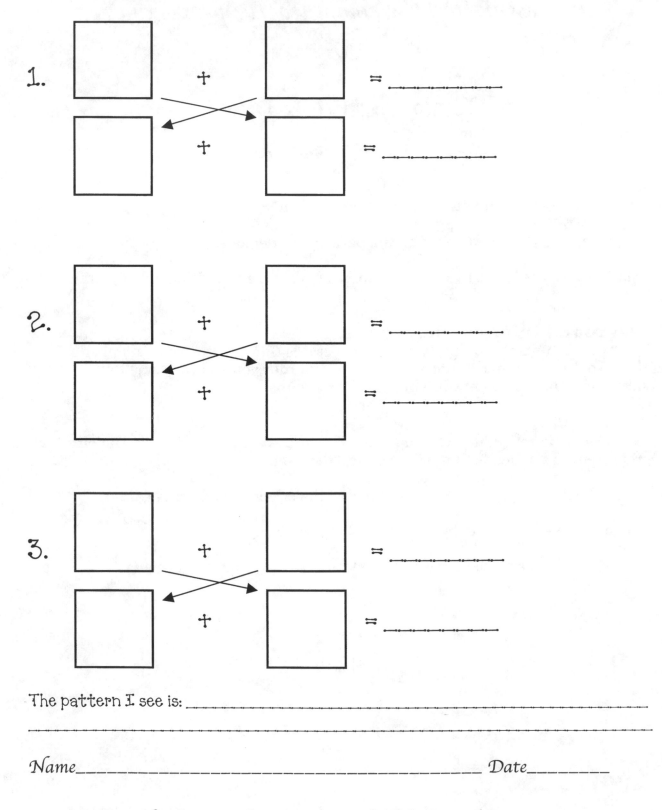

1. ☐ + ☐ = ...
   ☐ + ☐ = ...

2. ☐ + ☐ = ...
   ☐ + ☐ = ...

3. ☐ + ☐ = ...
   ☐ + ☐ = ...

The pattern I see is: ....

....

Name_____ Date_____

ADDITION CONCEPT:
Understanding the associative property of addition

Associative & Dice

Preparation:
- Duplicate the ***Associative Property of Addition*** worksheet (page 39) for each student.

- Provide each student with any 3 dice sets found on page 17.

- Make an overhead transparency of page 40 and overhead dice (see page 37 for instructions).

Background information:
The associative property of addition states that for any whole numbers a,b, and c, $(a+b)+c=a+(b+c)$. In other words, it doesn't matter which two of three numbers you add together first, the sum will always be the same.

Procedure:
- Students roll the dice placing each die on the worksheet.

- Instruct students to add the two dice in the parenthesis first and then add the third die.

- After recording the sum, slide the dice along the arrows and repeat the procedure.

- Upon completion of the worksheet, discuss the pattern of the associative property.

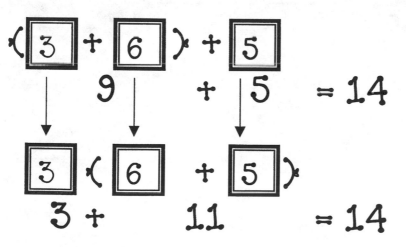

Associative Property of Addition

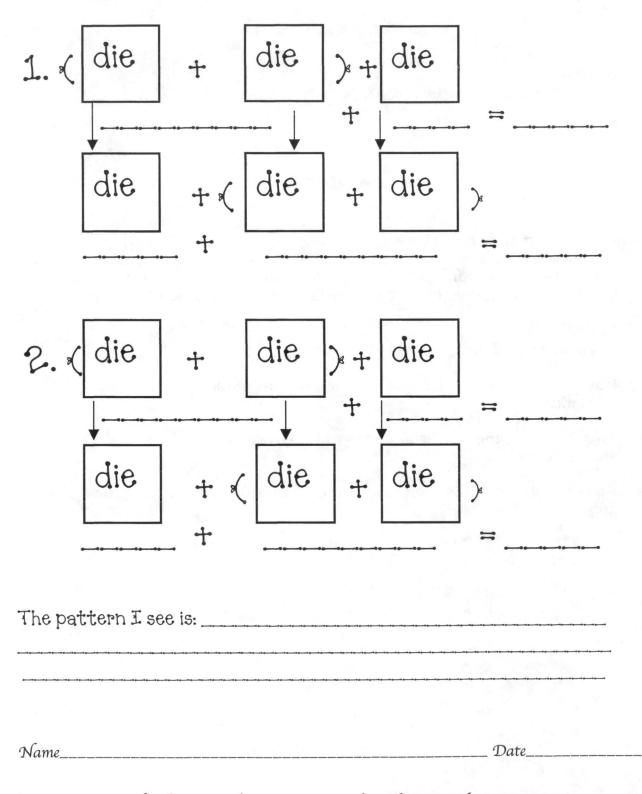

1. (die + die) + die
   die + (die + die)

   + =
   + + =

2. (die + die) + die
   die + (die + die)

   + =
   + + =

The pattern I see is: _____

_____

_____

Name_____ Date_____

Activities
For
Multi-Digit
Addition

Hundreds	Tens	Ones
▦	| |	O

ADDITION CONCEPT:
Understanding bases in preparation for multi-digit addition

Bases & Chips

Preparation:
- Provide 10-20 yellow, blue, green, and red chips per student. If commercial chips are not available, cut 1 inch squares of colored construction paper.

- Duplicate the trading board on page 45 for each student.

- Each student will need yellow, blue, green and red crayons, and one commercial die.

- Make an overhead transparency of page 45 and some overhead chips in yellow, green and red by using an overhead marker to color circles on acetate paper. Note that all these materials are available commercially.

Procedure:
- Instruct students to color the top of their trading boards according to the written color.

- Students need to separate their chips into piles according to the colors.

- Use the overhead materials to illustrate the concept of trading rates.

  Base four example:
  Using 4 as a trade rate, explain to the students that they cannot have 4 or more chips in any one column. Whenever they get 4 they must trade them in for the next color. Put 2 yellow chips on the overhead trading board. Add one...add another one...How many yellows do I have on my board in the yellow column? (4) By the rules of this game, this is illegal. I can't have 4 or more so what must I do? (trade for a blue chip). Continue this demonstration but call out numbers between 1-6 and ask students to tell you what you should do.

Instructions continue on page 44...

- When students understand how to trade, specify a trade rate. Tell students that every time you call out a number they are to take that specific amount in yellow chips. They will need to trade to keep their boards legal. Stop periodically and ask the class how many chips are represented on their boards. Continue until one red chip is put on the trading board. This initial learning experience works well with partners or small groups of students.

- Use other trade rates until students can trade quickly and see the relationships between the columns. This builds a solid foundation for working with base ten for multi-digit addition.

Hundreds	Tens	Ones
▦	‖	O

Chip Trading Board

Yellow	
Blue	
Green	
Red	

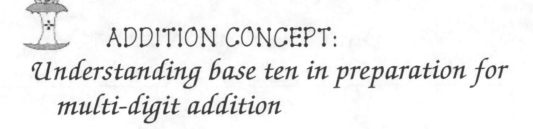

ADDITION CONCEPT:
Understanding base ten in preparation for multi-digit addition

Base Ten Trade and Bank It

Preparation:
- Provide each student with a commercial die and 10-20 yellow, blue, green, and red chips. If commercial chips are not available, cut 1 inch squares of colored construction paper.

- Duplicate the chip trading board on page 45 for each student.

Procedure:
- Divide students into groups of 4-5 players. Each group needs to select one player to be the "banker". The banker can be rotated each new game.

- The banker takes all the player's chips and sets up a "bank" on a trading board.

- The game is played just like the "Bases and Chips" activity on page 43 except that the trade rate will always be ten. Ten yellow chips must be traded for one blue chip, ten blue chips for one green chip, and ten green chips for one red. Players will roll the die to determine how many yellow chips they will place on their trading boards. The first player to reach one red chip wins the round and becomes the new banker.

- Encourage players to verbalize to the banker how many and what color of chips they need.

- Periodically go around and ask students to tell you what they have on their boards, i.e. 24=2 tens and 4 ones.

ADDITION CONCEPT:
Developing multi-digit addition with chip Trading

Joining Sets of Chips

Preparation:

- Distribute chip trading boards for each set of 2 students (page 45).

- Students will also need 2 commercial dice per group of 4 students, 10-20 yellow, blue, green, and red chips or 1 inch colored construction paper.

- Provide graph paper (page 20) to record addition problems.

Procedure:

- Divide students into groups of 4. Two students will partner up and play against the other two.

- Place all the chips in the center of the playing area on a trading board.

- Each player rolls one die and places that amount of yellow chips on their trading board. Partners then combine their collections, trading to make legal collections.

- Partners record their first sum on the graph paper.

Example of a play:

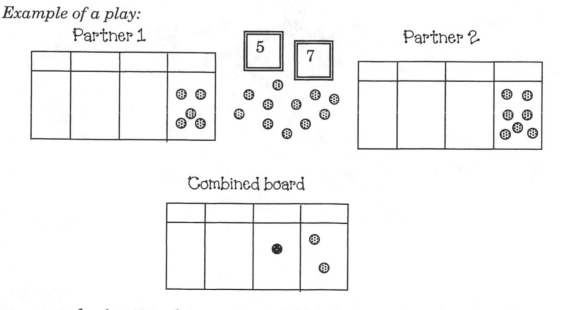

- Each time partners combine their collections, that total sum is added to the previous sum on their graph paper.
    Example:

				1	
				2	9
			+	1	6
				4	5

Previous Sum

New Round

New Sum

- Play continues until one team trades for a red chip.

ADDITION CONCEPT:
Developing multi-digit addition with and without regrouping

Add those beans

Preparation:
- Construct **Addition Trading boards** for each student (see instructions on page 51 .

- Have each student assemble a beanstick kit (see instructions on page 52).

- Duplicate the **Add those beans!** worksheet on page 54.

- Make overhead manipulatives by drawing an addition trading board with overhead markers. Copy the hundred flat pattern onto a transparency and use real beans and ten-sticks to illustrate the concepts.

Special note: *You may use* **baseten blocks** *if you don't want to invest in making Beansticks. They are actually better for 4-6th graders.*

Procedure:
1. Distribute a trading board, beansticks, and flats (real and cut out drawings) to each student.

2. Model the process of adding the ones – trading if necessary – and adding the tens using the overhead manipulatives. Students into groups of 4. Two students will partner up and play against the other two.

Example dialogue:
> *Show me 17 on your trading boards (1 ten and 7 ones).*
> *We are going to add 25 to that number (2 tens and 5 ones)*
> *Place 2 tens and 5 ones (loose beans) in the columns below the 17.*
> *Add the ones column by putting all the ones together.*
> *How many? (12: 1 ten and 2 ones)*
> *Remember, you can't have 10 or more in any column*
> *Trade if necessary.*
> *Add the tens column by bringing all the tens down.*
> *How many? 4 tens. The sum is 42*

Instructions continue on page 50…

3. Provide lots of opportunities for students to show and solve multi-digit addition problems either from textbooks or worksheets like page 53.

4. Progress to problems into the hundreds place. Once this foundation is built, it is not necessary to use the manipulatives for problems larger than the hundreds place. Students will be able to transfer the concept.

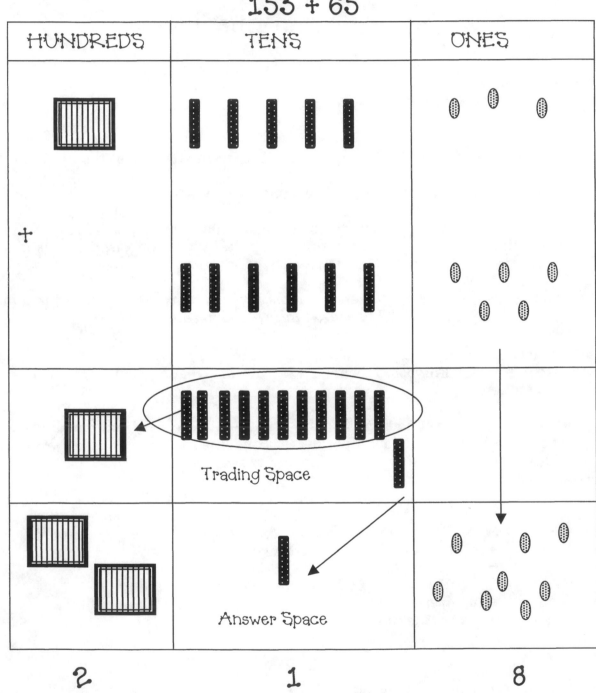

153 + 65

| HUNDREDS | TENS | ONES |

Trading Space

Answer Space

2   1   8

Addition Trading Board
Instructions for construction

Materials Needed:
- 45cm x 60cm white posterboard (1 per student)
- black permanent marker
- ruler

Construction:
Design the board according to the pattern below:

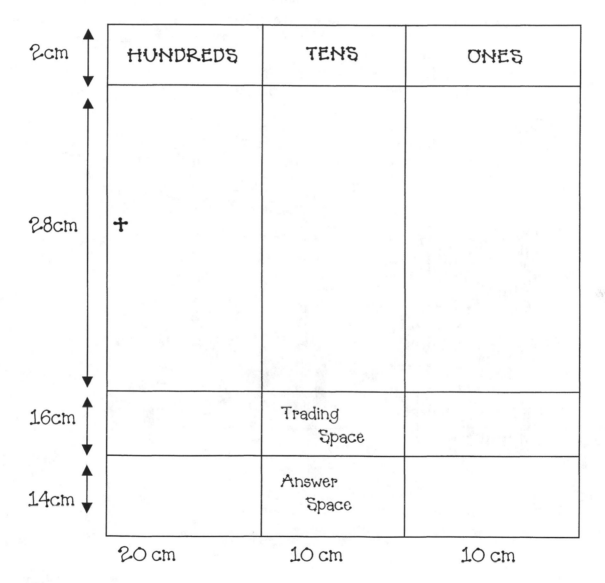

Special note: *Before laminating this, you may want to use the other side for a subtraction trading board (see instructions on page 134).*

Beansticks & Hundred-Bean Flats
Instructions for construction

Materials Needed:
- Small red beans
- Popscicle sticks
- White glue
- Heavy tagboard

Construction:

Ten-Beanstick: Apply white glue liberally to a popscicle stick and place 10 beans spaced evenly in the glue. Follow with a final gluing over the tops and in between the beans to prevent chipping. Let the glue dry for 24 hours before using.

Hundred-Bean Flat: Glue ten beansticks side by side onto heavy tagboard. Duplicate the hundred flat drawings pattern on page 52 to use for addition flats.

Student Beanstick set:

A set for 1 student consists of 1-2 real hundred-bean flats, 9 drawings of flats, 20 beansticks, and 20 loose beans. Store the set in reclosable bags.

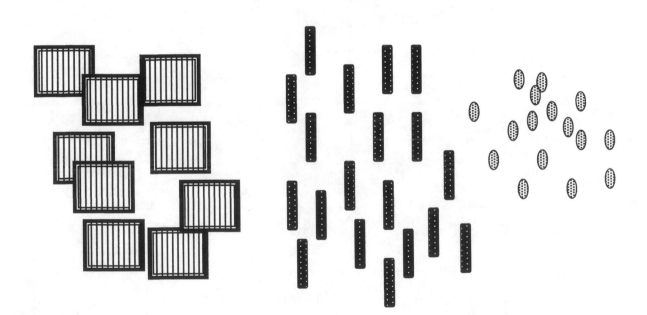

Hundred-Bean Flat Pattern
Duplicate on cardstock and cut apart individually

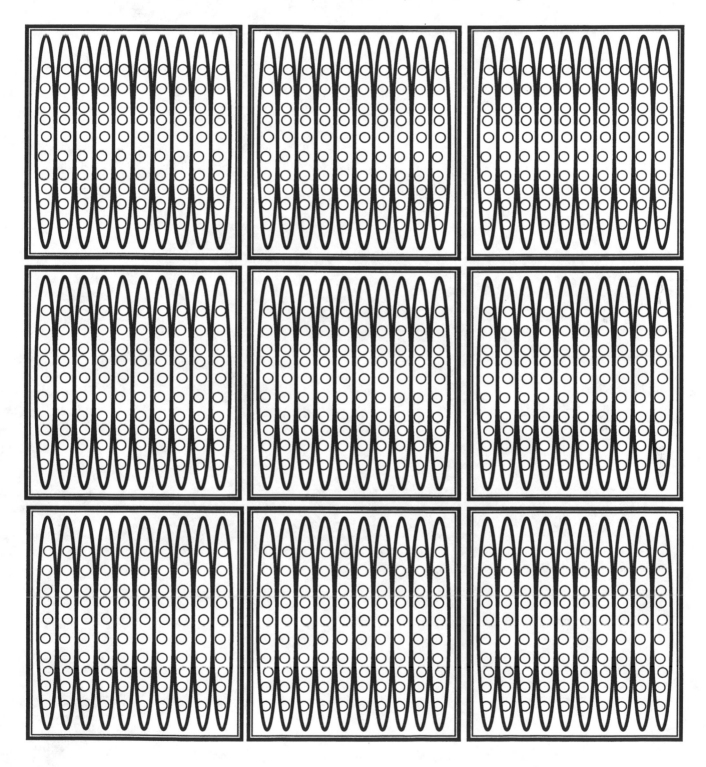

Add those beans

Use your beansticks and addition trading board to show and solve these addition problems.

1.　36
　 + 27

2.　53
　 + 64

3. 71
　 + 42

4.　68
　 + 49

5. 32
　 + 24

6. 62
　 + 23

7. 46
　 + 12

8.　54
　 + 23

9. 56
　 + 17

10. 49
　 + 35

11. 29
　 + 32

12. 16
　 + 47

13.　12
　 + 63

14.　47
　 + 22

15.　93
　 + 16

16.　134
　 + 21

17. 123
　 + 16

18. 130
　 + 69

19.　162
　 + 39

20. 110
　 + 123

21. 128
　 + 68

ADDITION CONCEPT:
Developing multi-digit addition using representational notation

Draw those beans

Preparation:

• Provide each student with a beanstick set (page 52-53).

• Duplicate pages 56-57 for each student.

• Use the overhead manipulatives created in Add Those Beans (page 48) and make overhead transparencies of pages 56-57.

Procedure:

1. Using the overhead manipulatives, illustrate several addition problems as you did in the Add Those Beans lesson on pages 49-50.
2. Instruct students to use the following system of notation that corresponds with the manipulatives:

Flats:	**Beansticks:**	**Beans:**
□	|	■

3. Distribute **Draw Those Beans** practice sheet (page 56) and illustrate with the overhead transparencies and manipulatives the first two problems. Let students complete the practice sheet to develop fluency with the notation system.
4. Use **Draw Those Beans** workmat (page 57) for students to practice a variety of addition problems that are found in their textbook or that you provide.

Example:

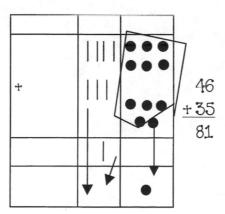

$$\begin{array}{r} 46 \\ +35 \\ \hline 81 \end{array}$$

Draw those beans

Practice Sheet

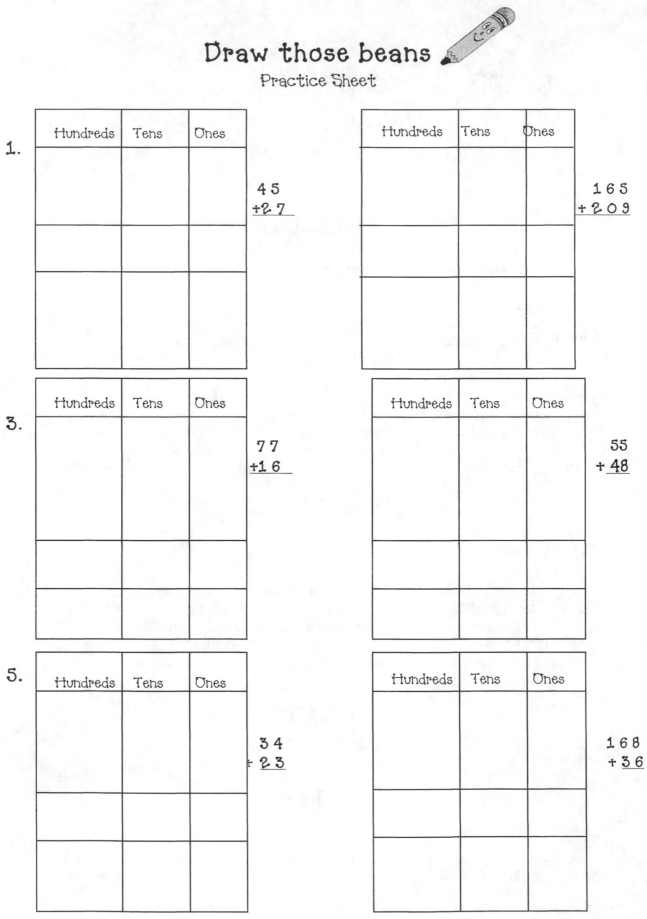

1.

Hundreds	Tens	Ones

45
+27

Hundreds	Tens	Ones

165
+209

3.

Hundreds	Tens	Ones

77
+16

Hundreds	Tens	Ones

55
+48

5.

Hundreds	Tens	Ones

34
+23

Hundreds	Tens	Ones

168
+36

Draw those beans

Workmat

1.

Hundreds	Tens	Ones

2.

Hundreds	Tens	Ones

3.

Hundreds	Tens	Ones

4.

Hundreds	Tens	Ones

5.

Hundreds	Tens	Ones

6.

Hundreds	Tens	Ones

ADDITION CONCEPT:
Developing multi-digit addition using without those beans!

No Beans Please!

Preparation:
• Provide each student with a copy of the workmat on page 59.

Procedure:
• Using the workmat, students will write the representational notation learned on page 55 to solve various addition problems generated by the teacher or textbook.

HUNDRED s	TENS	ONES

55
+37

92

• If students experience problems using the notation without the beans, let them validate their answers with the beans.

No Beans Please!

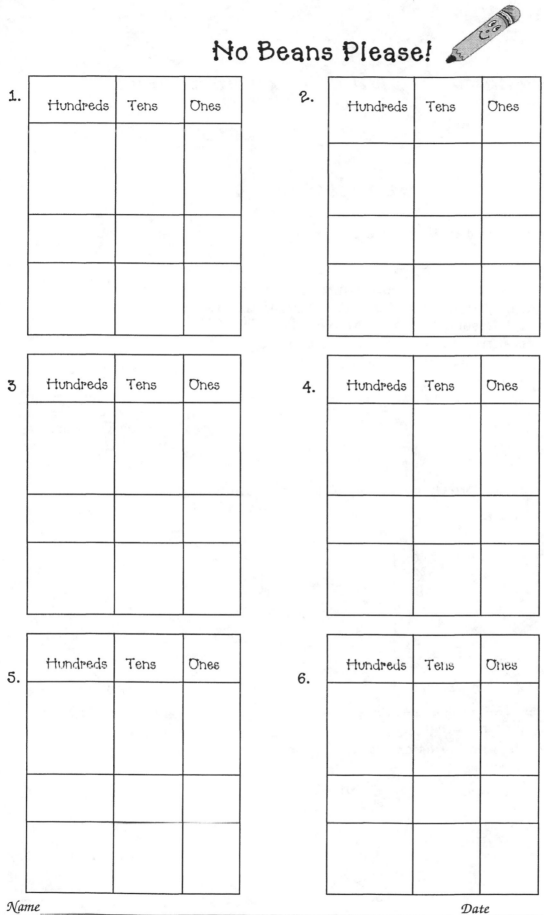

1.

Hundreds	Tens	Ones

2.

Hundreds	Tens	Ones

3.

Hundreds	Tens	Ones

4.

Hundreds	Tens	Ones

5.

Hundreds	Tens	Ones

6.

Hundreds	Tens	Ones

Name_____ Date_____

ADDITION CONCEPT:
Practicing multi-digit addition up through 10 digits

Palindrome It

Preparation:
• Distribute a copy of **Palindrome It!** (page 60) to each student.

Background Information:

A palindrome is a word or number (in this case a number) that reads the same forward and backward. i.e., pop, tot, toot, radar, 101, 2112, 23232, 111. Palindromes can also be complete sentences. i.e., "Madam, I'm adam."

A most interesting aspect of the numerical palindrome is the way in which it can be derived. Pick any number, reverse it, and add the two. *Example:*

$$\begin{array}{r} 421 \\ +124 \\ \hline 545 \end{array}$$

The result is a Palindrome.

Sometimes it takes more than one step as in this example:

$$\begin{array}{r} 273 \\ +\ 372 \\ \hline 645 \\ +\ 546 \\ \hline 1191 \\ +1911 \\ \hline 3102 \\ +2013 \\ \hline 5115 \end{array}$$

Special note: This will always work! You can use any number and eventually you will reach a palindrome. This activity is a fascinating way to take the traditionally dull routine of drill and practice out of addition problems. *Warning:* A calculator may be handy if you try 89!

Procedure:
• Provide the background information on palindromes to the students before they complete the **Palindrome It** worksheet on page 61.

Palindrome It!

1. 435

2. 135

3. 361

4. 497

5. 251

6. 291

Try some of your own

7.

8.

9.

Bonus: Try all the numbers 1-100 and make a chart of how many steps each took.

Name_____ Date_____

ADDITION CONCEPT:
Reinforcing multi-digit addition with two-digit Numerals

Sideways Dominoes

Preparation:
- Supply each student with a set of Double-Six dominoes
- Each student will need a copy of **Sideways Dominoes** (page 63).

Procedure:
1. Explain to the students that they will work with their dominoes turned sideways to form tens and ones.
2. Assign each student a target number (see list below). Using twelve dominoes, students try and find 6 different ways to express the target number (sum). Students use the worksheet on page 63 to record their solutions.

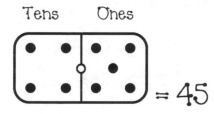

Tens   Ones   = 45

List of target numbers that have 6 solutions:

No regrouping involved:
16,17,24,25,26,27,28,29,34,35,36,37,38,39,43,44,45,46,47,48,49,52,53,54,55,56,57
58,59,61,62,63,64,65,66,67,68,69,72,73,74,75,76,77,78,79,82,83,84,85,86,87,88,89
92,93,94,95,96,97,98,103,104,105,106,107

Regrouping involved:
30,31,40,41,42,50,51,60,61,70,80,81,90,91,101,102

Sideways Dominoes

Target Number _____

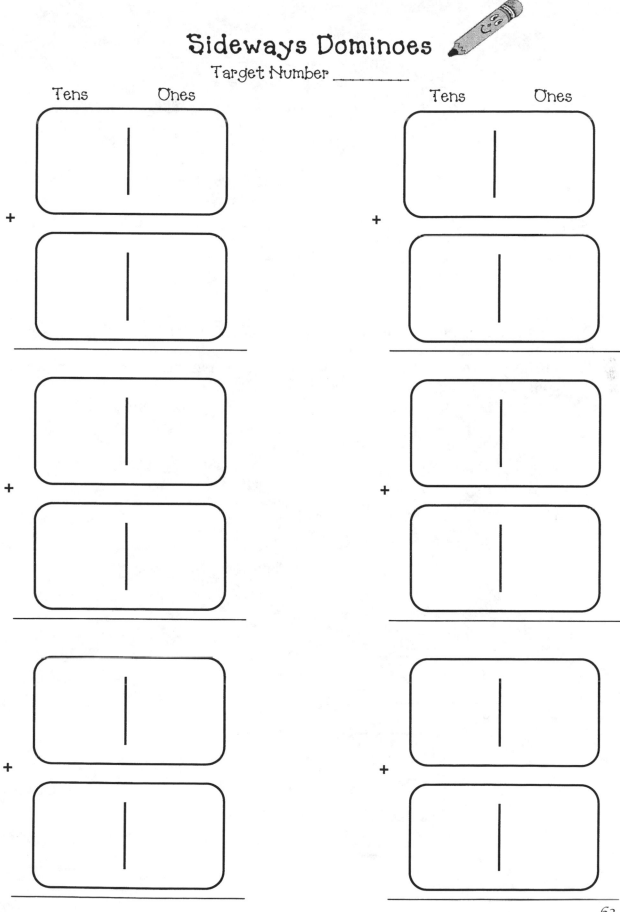

ADDITION CONCEPT:
Practicing multi-digit addition with dominoes

Domino Marathon

Preparation:
- Supply each student with a set of Double-Nine dominoes. Remove the blank domino from each set.
- Each student will need a copy of the ***Domino Marathon*** worksheets (pages 65-66).

Procedure:
- Students use 27 dominoes to form 9 complete addition problems. Remind students that the dominoes can only be used once.
- To facilitate correcting, have students correct their partners paper and rate them using the following scale:

# of problems solved	Title earned
1	Scooter
2	Crawler
3	Walker
4	Jogger
5	Runner
6	Dasher
7	Sprinter
8	Marathoner
9	Mega Marathoner

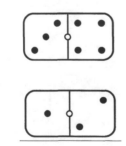

\+

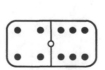

Domino Marathon

Create as many correct addition problems as you can. You may not use a domino twice.

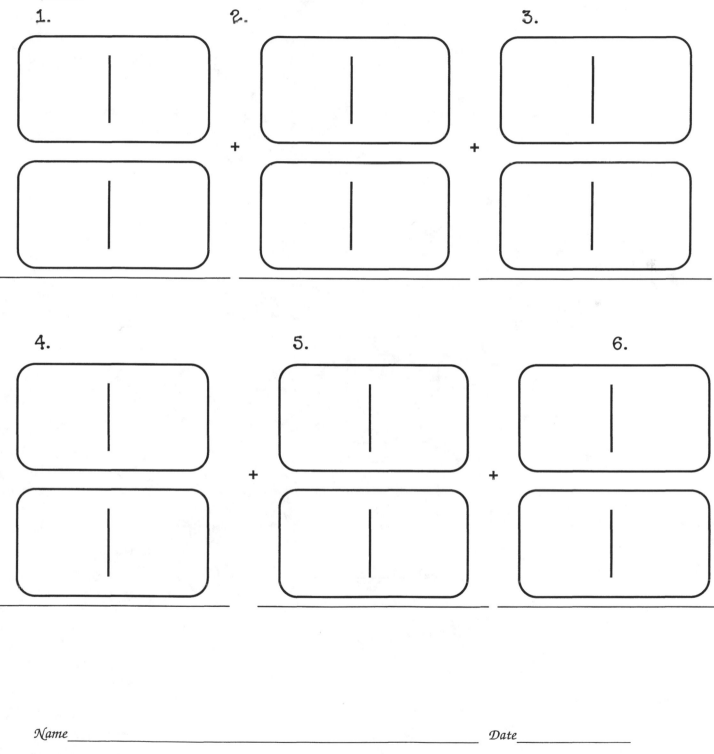

1.

+

2.

+

3.

+

4.

+

5.

+

6.

+

Name_____ Date_____

Domino Marathon
(continued)

7.

8.

+

+

9.

+

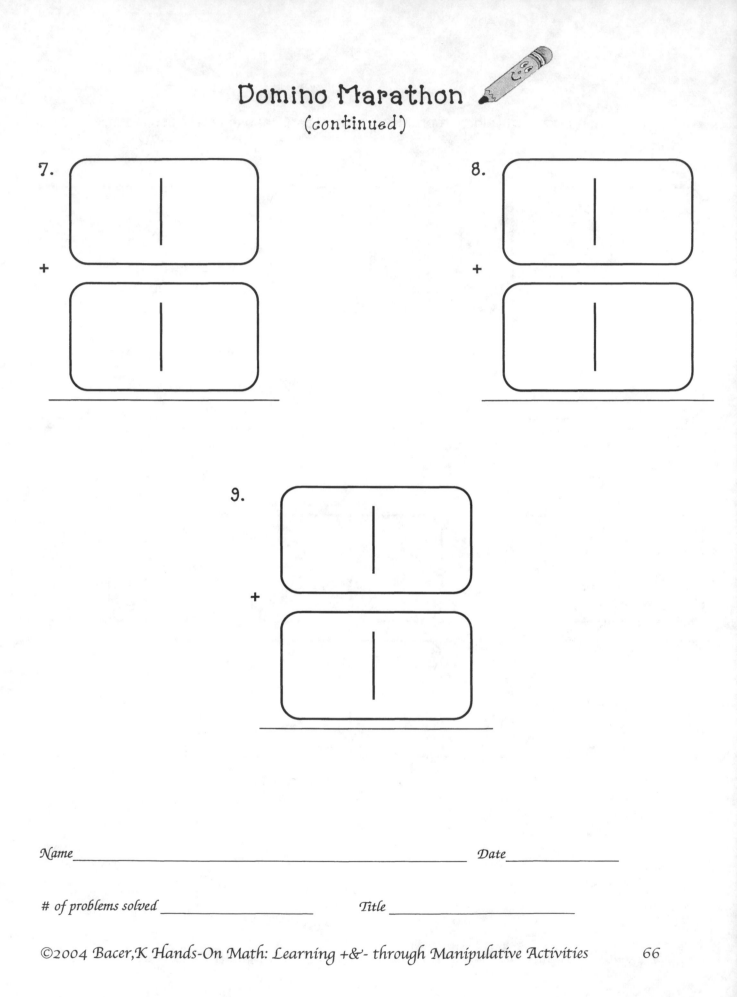

Name_____ Date_____

# of problems solved _____   Title _____

ADDITION CONCEPT:
Reinforcing multi-digit addition with dominoes

Domino Mania

Preparation:
- Supply each student with a set of Double-Nine dominoes.
- Reproduce the various domino worksheets from pages 68-74.

Procedure:
Select the appropriate domino worksheet for each student.

Special Instructions for each worksheet:

Domino Magic Squares Warm-up – Students do not need dominoes for this worksheet. Add the dominoes horizontally and vertically to reach the boxed sum.

Domino Magic Squares – Dominoes are used to solve each magic square puzzle. Dominoes can only be used once.

Double Magic Squares Warm-up - Students do not need dominoes for this worksheet. Add the dominoes horizontally, vertically and diagonally to find the sum.

Double Magic Squares – Students use dominoes to solve each double magic square puzzle. Dominoes can only be used once.

Double Magic Mystery Squares – Students use dominoes and the clues given to find the dominoes that will solve the double magic mystery number.

Square Domino Sums – Dominoes are placed so that they horizontally and vertically they equal the sum in the middle of the domino square.

Domino Maze – Specific dominoes are used to solve this puzzle. Each row and column must equal 14 when completed.

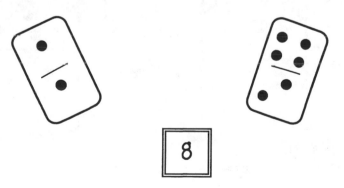

Domino Magic Square Warm-up

Add both ways and record the sum.

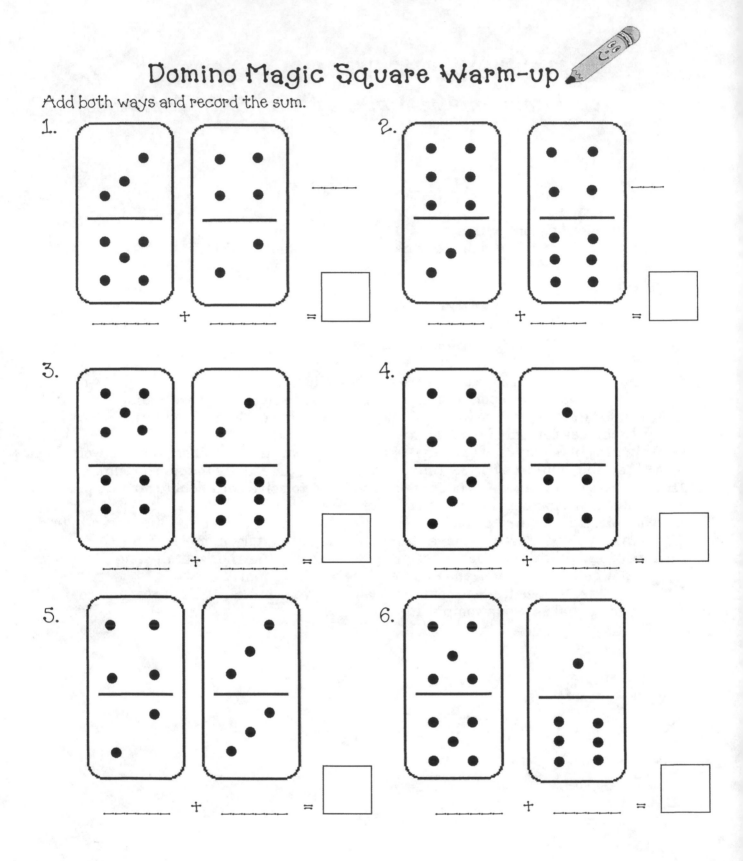

Domino Magic Squares

Find the dominoes that solve the magic squares. Record the results.

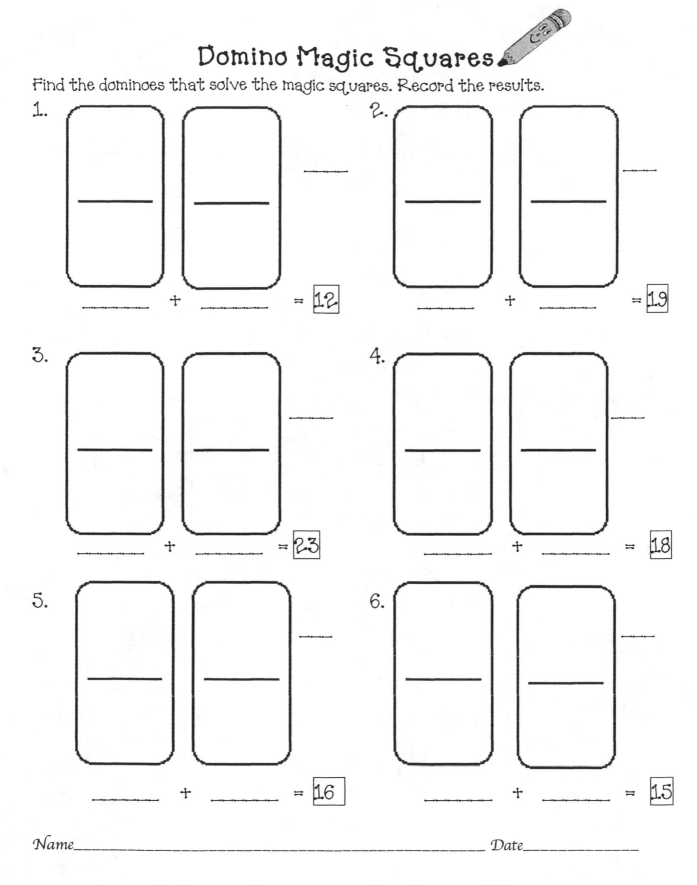

1. _____ + _____ = 12

2. _____ + _____ = 19

3. _____ + _____ = 23

4. _____ + _____ = 18

5. _____ + _____ = 16

6. _____ + _____ = 15

Name_____ Date_____

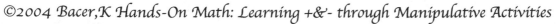

Double Magic Squares Warm-up

Add three ways and record the sums. Magic Sum goes in large square.

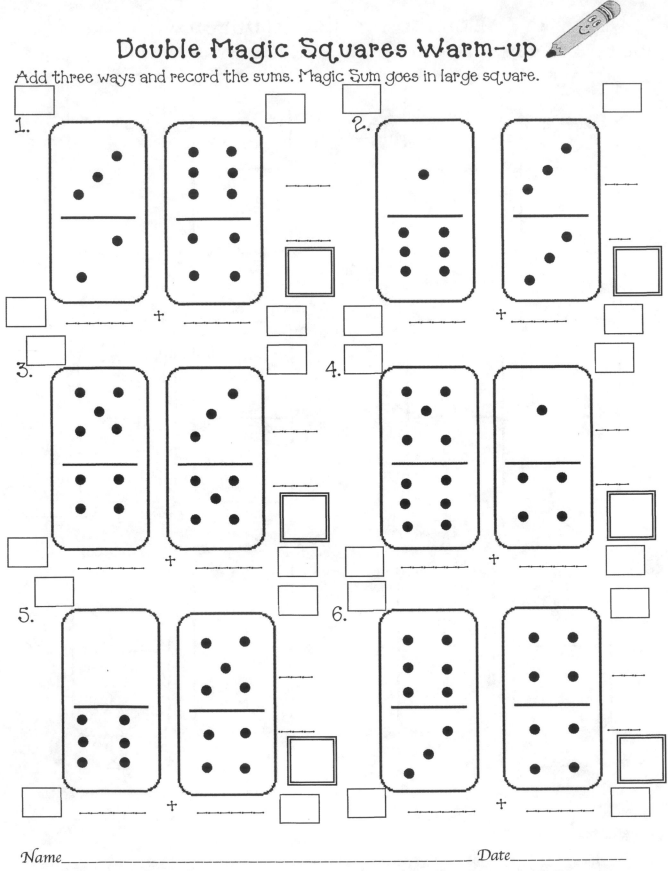

Double Magic Squares

Find dominoes to create a magic sum all three ways. Record the results

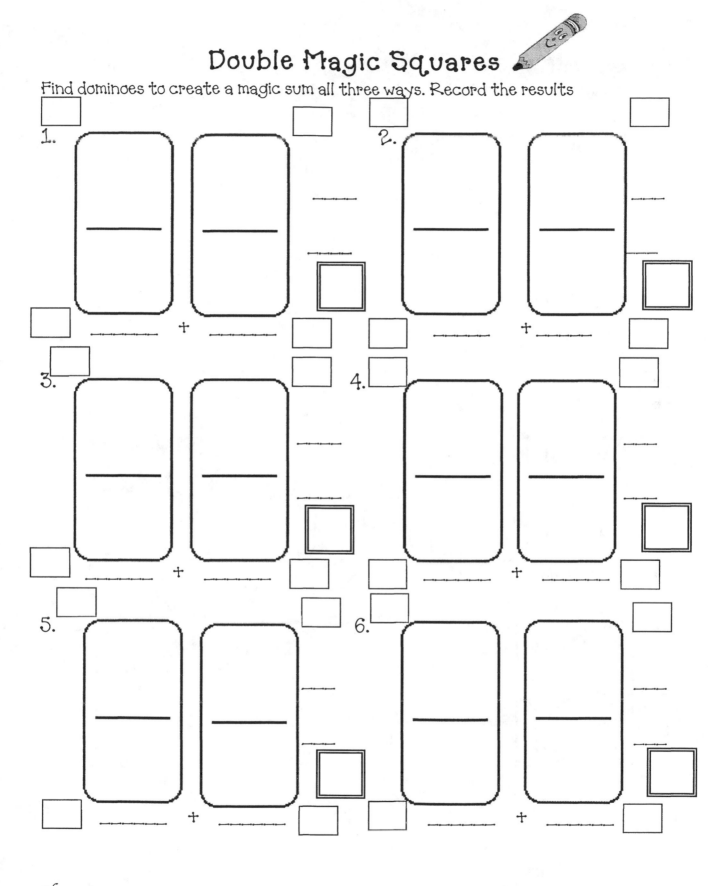

Name_____ Date_____

©2004 Bacer,K Hands-On Math: Learning +&- through Manipulative Activities

Double Magic Square Mystery Squares

Find the dominoes that solve the magic squares. Record the results.

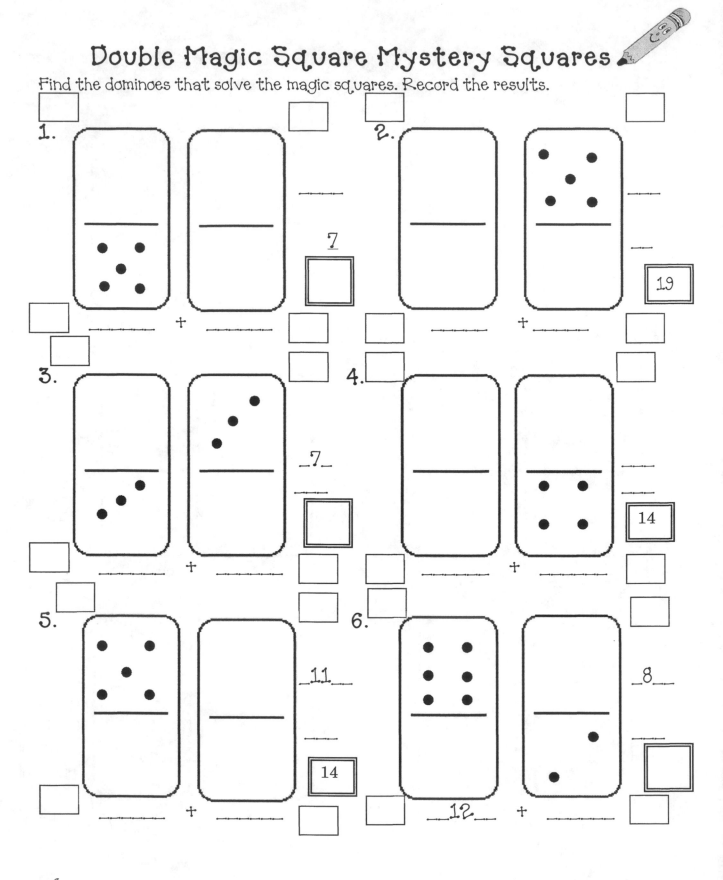

Name_____ Date_____

Square Domino Sums

Place dominoes in each square so that the horizontal and vertical sums are the same as the number in the middle of the square.

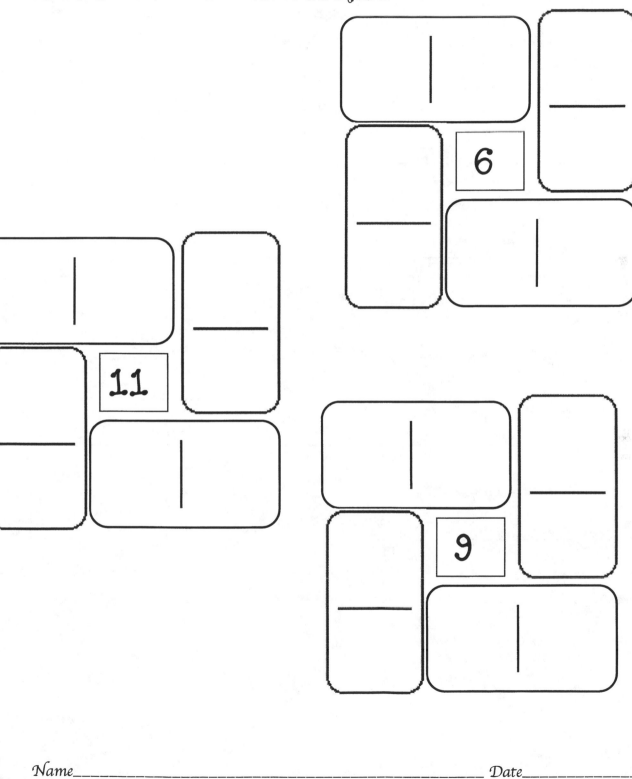

Domino Maze

Find these dominoes from your set:

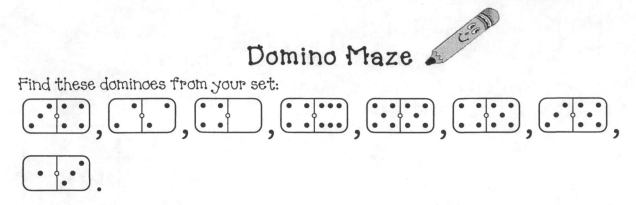

Place the dominoes in the maze so that each row and column add up to 14.

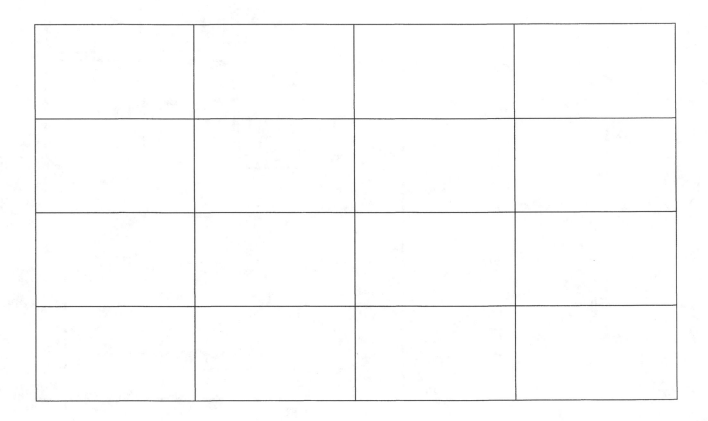

ADDITION CONCEPT:
Managing large multi-digit addition problems

Sum Graph

Preparation:
- Provide graph paper for each student.
- Make an overhead transparency of the graph paper for illustration purposes.
- Duplicate a **Sum Graph** worksheet (page 76) for each student.

Procedure:
- Graph paper is an excellent manipulative for managing large addition problems.
- Illustrate on the overhead projector how the graph paper is used to keep each column neatly organized.

Example: **1,562 + 473**

		1	1		
		1	5	6	2
	+		4	7	3
	2	0	3	5	

- Provide lots of practice with a variety of problems using graph paper to manage the columns.

Sum Graph

Use Graph paper to solve the following problems:

1. 4,672
    +   549

2. 3,276
    +4,602

3. 1,465
    +2,734

4. 6,474
    +3,761

5. 56,473
    + 4,982

6. 31,705
    + 5,921

7. 495,637
    + 46,321

8. 509,342
    +650,471

9. 600,001
    +702,569

10. 143,265
    +459,124

11. 369,250
    +105,692

12. 654,098
    +123,456

♥Bonus   3,712,469,872
        +   987,654,321

Don't forget to staple your graph paper to this worksheet.

Name_____ Date_____

©2004 Bacer,K Hands-On Math: Learning +&- through Manipulative Activities

Subtraction Basics for Educators

What do I owe?

Do I have enough?

Take a Ten

Pay Debts

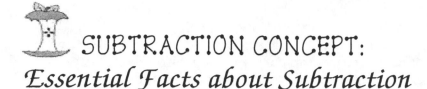

SUBTRACTION CONCEPT:
Essential Facts about Subtraction

Subtraction Basics for the Educator

> **Subtraction** - that notorious mathematical operation that suddenly causes the first signs of math anxiety in elementary students.

Those elementary students were probably confident in addition, so what happens when they encounter subtraction? Many educators say that the reason students have difficulty with subtraction is linked to their weak foundation in addition. It that really the cause though?

In subtraction the whole and one part are given. The unknown part is to be found. Sound confusing? For an elementary student – yes! Subtraction is an inverse operation. Suddenly we are asking students to take their addition foundation and think backwards! When multi-digit subtraction is encountered, we ask them to break a very important base ten mathematical concept – we suddenly tell them it is acceptable to have 16 in the ones column after borrowing. Why? Tradition?

The purpose of this next section is to provide educators with a mathematically sound alternative to the problems encountered in subtraction. A subtraction though process will be presented that will allow the student "think through" the subtraction process. The method I have developed may not be the traditional method, but it is mathematically sound and I have witnessed students with all different mathematical abilities master the largest subtraction problems after learning only six basic facts and establishing a very simple "subtraction thinking" strategy.

It is my desire that you will be challenged to break tradition and develop a whole new meaning to subtraction for yourself as a mathematician and for your students as budding mathematicians.

Background Information:

To be able to effectively teach the remaining activities in this book, an understanding of my subtraction method is necessary. It is based on the same mathematical concept that is used in addition. It is important for you as a mathematics educator to have a solid base ten foundation.

What comes after 9 ones? 10 ones? No – 1 ten. Take a close look at ten.

1 0

Mathematically it is 1 ten and 0 ones.

In addition we teach students that they can't have more than 9 ones in the ones place (base ten principle), 9 tens in the tens place, and so on through the columns. From this concept we develop carrying, regrouping, or renaming. When subtraction is taught, this important base ten concept is suddenly changed. Borrowing takes place and then we teach that it is find to have for example, 14 ones in the ones column. Mathematically there 14 ones does not exist. It is 1 ten and 4 ones!

Prerequisite Skills:

Six facts are all that is needed as a prerequisite skill! Say good-bye to finger counting and students who just can not memorize basic subtraction facts. The six facts are:

0 + 10 = 10
1 + 9 = 10
2 + 8 = 10
3 + 7 = 10
4 + 6 = 10
5 + 5 = 10

Using the commutative property, these facts will also be known as:

10 + 0 = 10
9 + 1 = 10
8 + 2 = 10
7 + 3 = 10
6 + 4 = 10
5 + 5 = 10

The activities on pages 83-92 will provide development and reinforcement of these essential facts.

The Thought Process:

Once students are able to think through a subtraction thought process, the famous "Do we have to borrow on this page?" question will no longer be asked.

In subtraction we take the minuend from the subtrahend. From now on think of the minuend as a **debt – what is owed.** Teach students to box the debt in red.

Example:

$$2\ 7$$
$$-\ 9$$

The thought process has five easy steps. Memorize them.

Step 1 – *"What do I owe?*   9
     Box debt in red

Step 2 – *"Do I have enough?*
     No, I only have 7. If yes, skip to step 3.

Step 3 – *"Take a ten."*
Don't borrow unless you plan on giving it back!
Don't steal, it's not nice!

So…take a ten. Here's the trick – when you take the ten take it according to your debt and what is left.
Example:

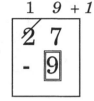

Step 4 – *"Pay debts!"* Cross off the debt.

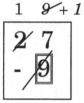

Step 5 – *"What's left? "* 8.

This thought process is repeated for each column. The process eliminates students doing haphazard borrowing without even knowing if they need to! You can also use the steps for traditional subtraction. It forces students to **think through** subtraction.

Teach the thought process with simple problems and then progress to harder problems.
Some examples:

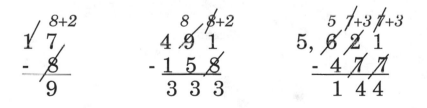

After working with a variety of simple problems, students will start using mental math. Showing their work may progress like this...

$$
\begin{array}{r}
2 \quad 53 \ 4 \\
\cancel{3} \ \cancel{6} \ 5 \\
- \quad \underline{7 \ 6} \\
2 \ 8 \ 9
\end{array}
$$

Notice the student thought of the debt mentally and just jotted what was left of the debt.

Keep in mind that you have probably done subtraction the traditional way for a long time – practice this way and you will notice (especially if you had a hard time memorizing those subtraction facts) that you can do very large problems very quickly. It is actually fun!

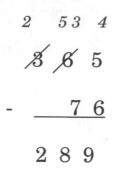

Activities for basic Subtraction Skills

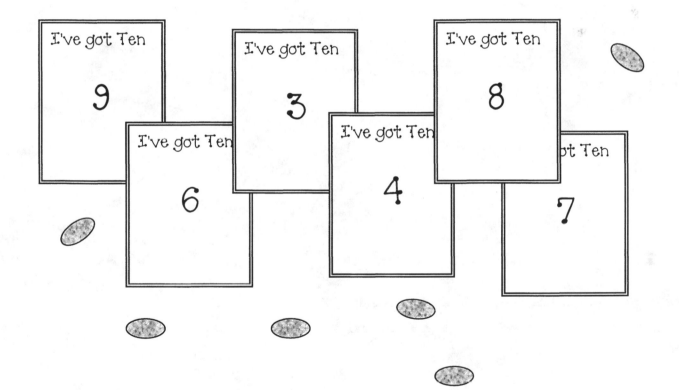

SUBTRACTION CONCEPT:
Developing sums of ten in preparation for subtraction

Shake Those Beans

Preparation:
- Spray paint one side of a bag of lima beans red or purchase two-sided counters. Empty film canisters work great for storing a set of 10 beans.

- Each student needs 10 lima beans and a small paper cup

- Duplicate the **Shake Those Beans** (page 86) worksheet for each student.

Procedure:
1. Divide students into groups of two.

2. Ten beans are placed in the small paper cup, shook, and dumped into the center of the playing area.

3. The beans that land with the red side up are counted as the first addend and the beans that land with the white side up are counted as the second addend.

4. Students fill in the square that matches the correct addition sentence on each shake/turn.

5. Partners alternate taking turns and the first partner to reach the top of a column wins.   *Example:*

0+10	1 + 9	2 +8	3 +7	4 + 6

Shake those Beans

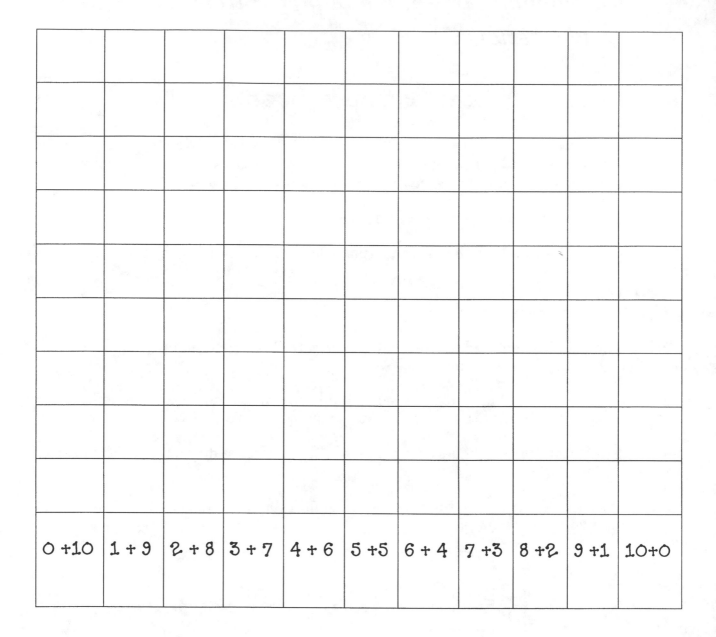

0 +10	1 + 9	2 + 8	3 + 7	4 + 6	5 +5	6 + 4	7 +3	8 +2	9 +1	10+0

Name _____ Date _____

SUBTRACTION CONCEPT:
Developing sums of ten in preparation for subtraction

I've got Ten

Preparation:
- Duplicate pages 88-91 onto cardstock. Cut out the set to make a deck of **"I've got ten** cards. Each group of 4 students will need a complete set.

- For students who can read, duplicate the **"thinking process cards"** (page 91) and include them with the **"I've got ten"** set.

Procedure:
- Divide students into groups of 4 players.

- 5 cards are dealt to each player and the remaining cards are placed face down in the center of the playing area.

- Player with the highest card or two highest cards goes first.

- The object of the game is to create sets of two cards that equal ten. On a player's turn any sets of ten are laid down in the front of their playing area. They may ask one player for a number which can be added to one of their cards to create a set of ten.

- If the player has the card asked for, they must give it to the player. If not they say, "take a card."

- Play continues until one player can play all their cards. Ten points are earned for each set of ten laid down.

- Encourage students to verbalize the sets of tens and thinking process cards.

Use of *thinking process* cards:
- The *thinking process* cards are played just like the sets of ten. There are two sets of matching cards in a deck.

I've Got Ten Cards

I've got ten	I've got ten	I've got ten	I've got ten	I've got ten	I've got ten
O	O	O	O	O	O
I've got ten	I've got ten	I've got ten	I've got ten	I've got ten	I've got ten
1	1	1	1	1	1
I've got ten	I've got ten	I've got ten	I've got ten	I've got ten	I've got ten
2	2	2	2	2	2
I've got ten	I've got ten	I've got ten	I've got ten	I've got ten	I've got ten
3	3	3	3	3	3

I've Got Ten Cards

I've got ten	I've got ten	I've got ten	I've got ten	I've got ten	I've got ten
4	4	4	4	4	4
I've got ten	I've got ten	I've got ten	I've got ten	I've got ten	I've got ten
5	5	5	5	5	5
I've got ten	I've got ten	I've got ten	I've got ten	I've got ten	I've got ten
6	6	6	6	6	6
I've got ten	I've got ten	I've got ten	I've got ten	I've got ten	I've got ten
7	7	7	7	7	7

I've Got Ten Cards

I've got ten	I've got ten	I've got ten	I've got ten	I've got ten	I've got ten
8	8	8	8	8	8
I've got ten	**I've got ten**	**I've got ten**	**I've got ten**	**I've got ten**	**I've got ten**
9	9	9	9	9	9
I've got ten	**I've got ten**	**I've got ten**	**I've got ten**	**I've got ten**	**I've got ten**
10	10	10	10	10	10
I've got ten	**I've got ten**	**I've got ten**	**I've got ten**	**I've got ten**	**I've got ten**

Thinking Process Cards

I've got ten What do I Owe?	I've got ten What do I Owe?	I've got ten What do I Owe?	I've got ten What do I Owe?	I've got ten What do I Owe?	I've got ten What do I Owe?
I've got ten Do I have enough?	I've got ten Do I have enough?	I've got ten Do I have enough?	I've got ten Do I have enough?	I've got ten Do I have enough?	I've got ten Do I have enough?
I've got ten Take a Ten	I've got ten Take a Ten	I've got ten Take a Ten	I've got ten Take a Ten	I've got ten Take a Ten	I've got ten Take a Ten
I've got ten Pay Debts!	I've got ten Pay Debts!	I've got ten Pay Debts!	I've got ten Pay Debts!	I've got ten Pay Debts!	I've got ten Pay Debts!
I've got ten What's left?	I've got ten What's left?	I've got ten What's left?	I've got ten What's left?	I've got ten What's left?	I've got ten What's left?

SUBTRACTION CONCEPT:
Developing sums of ten in preparation for subtraction

Spin Out

Preparation:

• Copy the spinner pattern(page 93) onto cardstock and assemble per instructions.

• Duplicate the gameboard on page 94. Each pair of students will need one board.

• Distribute 20 transparent chips (2 colors) per 2 students.

Procedure:

• Divide students into groups of two.

• Each player takes 10 transparent chips (same color per player).

• A turn consists of a spin and placing a transparent marker on the number square that will equal ten. For example, if 2 is spun a marker can be placed on any unoccupied 8 space.

• The player to get 6 markers diagonally, vertically, or horizontally first wins.

• If all the squares are filled before there is a winner, the game goes into overtime. In overtime a marker can be taken off an opponent's square that will create a sum of ten and the player can play their marker in that space.

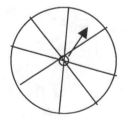 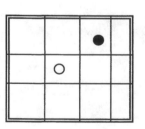

Spinner

Copy the spinner onto cardstock. Thread a brad through the small circle of a safety pin and then through the cardstock. The safety pin becomes the spinner.

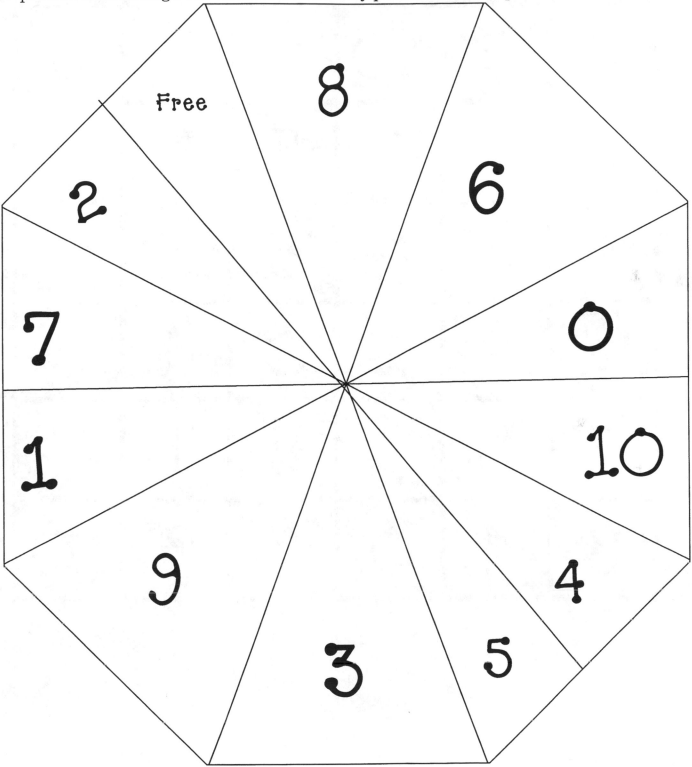

Spin Out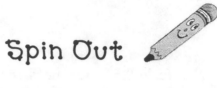

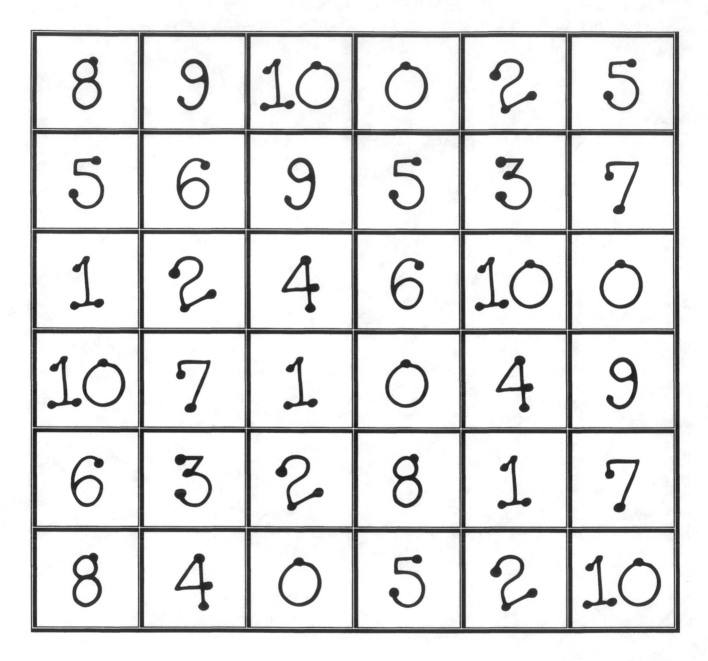

8	9	10	0	2	5
5	6	9	5	3	7
1	2	4	6	10	0
10	7	1	0	4	9
6	3	2	8	1	7
8	4	0	5	2	10

Activities for Subtraction Facts with Minuends to 9

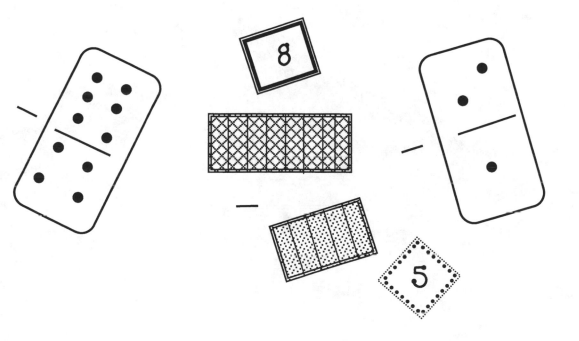

SUBTRACTION CONCEPT:
Developing basic subtraction facts with minuends to 9

Unifix It

Preparation:

- Duplicate the workmat on page 99 for each student.

- Supply each student with 2 sets of 9 unifix cubes – each a different color.

- Students will need crayons the same color as their unifix cubes.

- Using a permanent marker, write the following numerals on two 1 cm wooden cubes which will become a die:

  1ˢᵗ die– 1,2,3,4,5,6,   **2ⁿᵈ die** – 1,2,3,3,3,3

- Make an overhead transparency of page 99 and obtain a set of overhead markers the same colors as the unifix cubes. .

Procedure:

- Using the ***Unifix it*** overhead transparency (page 99) and markers, demonstrate the following:

   1. Roll the two dice and take that number in one color of unifix cubes.

   2. Repeat this process with the other color of unifix cubes.

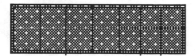 

   3. Use the longer set of unifix cubes first. Color in the first "What I have" section of the workmat (page 98) to match the unifix set. Record this numeral.

1	2	3	4	5	6	7	8	9	10	Numeral
What I have										7

4. The shorter set becomes the debt. Color the "debt" section to match the unifix cubes. Once again record the numeral.

	1	2	3	4	5	6	7	8	9	10	Numeral
Debt	▨	▨	▨	▨	▨						5

5. Demonstrate taking the debt away. Color in what is left on the workmat.

	1	2	3	4	5	6	7	8	9	10	Numeral
What I have	▨	▨	▨	▨	▨	▨	▨				7
Debt	▨	▨	▨	▨	▨						5
What is left	▨	▨									2

6. Activity continues with students using their dice and unifix cubes to complete the workmat on page 99.

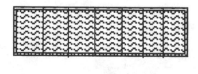

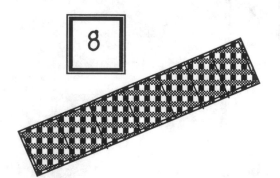

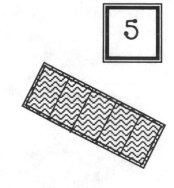

Unifix It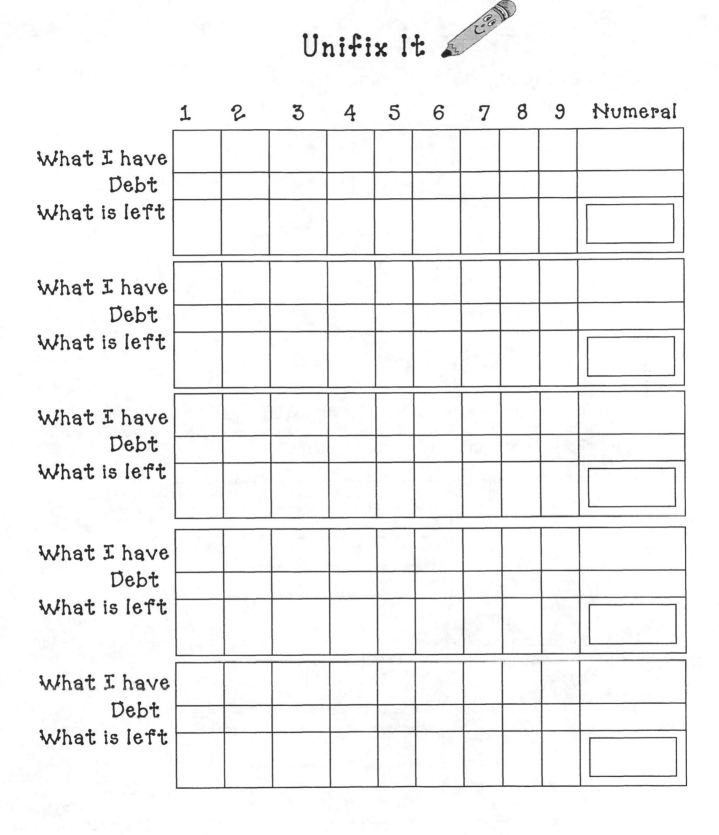

	1	2	3	4	5	6	7	8	9	Numeral
What I have										
Debt										
What is left										
What I have										
Debt										
What is left										
What I have										
Debt										
What is left										
What I have										
Debt										
What is left										
What I have										
Debt										
What is left										

Name_____ Date_____

SUBTRACTION CONCEPT:
Developing basic subtraction facts with minuends to 9

Graphic Relief

Preparation:
Supply each student with the following materials:
- 2-3 sheets of graph paper (page 102) or use commercial graph paper. Select a suitable size for the students' ability.
- red and black crayon
- scissors
- glue
- blank paper

Procedure:
- Students will use the graph paper to illustrate various subtraction problems. Using the black crayon, students will outline 9 different lengths of squares on the graph paper. They cannot outline more than 9 squares.

    Example:

- Using the red crayon students color in various amounts inside the black outlined strips . This will become the debts (what is owed).

    Example:

- Instruct students to cut out their strips and glue all their different problems on blank paper.
- Students then give their paper to a partner who writes the subtraction sentences of each problem and the answer.

   Example:

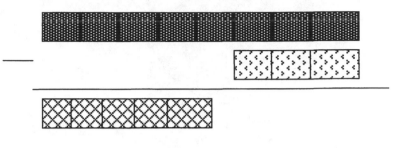

$$8-3=5$$

Special Note: This activity can easily be extended to cover all the basic subtraction facts.

One-Inch Graph Paper

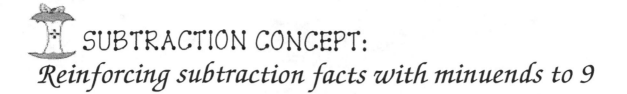
Domino Match-up

Preparation:
- Provide each student with a Double-Nine domino set (page 6,22)
- Duplicate the workmats on pages 104-106 for each student
- Create an overhead set of Double-Nine dominoes (instructions are on page 5)

Procedure:
- Illustrate with the overhead dominoes how to read a domino as a subtraction problem.

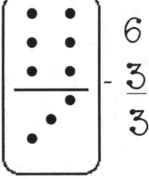

- Remind students that the larger number must always be on the top of the domino.

- The workmats on pages 104-106 provide reinforcement. Students place their dominoes in the correct categories.

Domino Match-up

Find all the dominoes with a different of O (there are ten) Draw them.

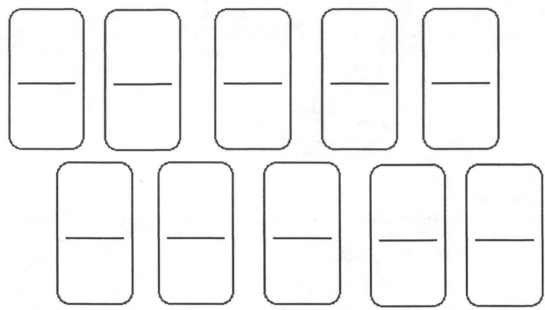

Find all the dominoes with a different of 1 (there are 9) Draw them.

Domino Match-up
(continued)

Find all the dominoes with a different of 2 (there are 8) Draw them.

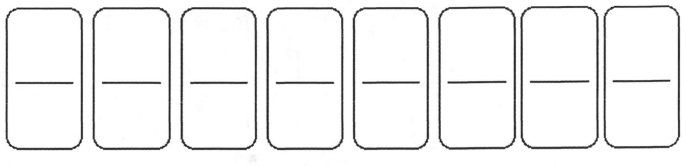

Find all the dominoes with a different of 3 (there are 7) Draw them.

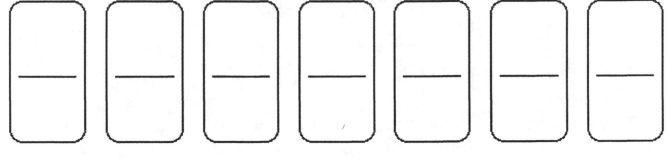

Find all the dominoes with a different of 4 (there are 6) Draw them.

Find all the dominoes with a different of 5 (there are 5) Draw them.

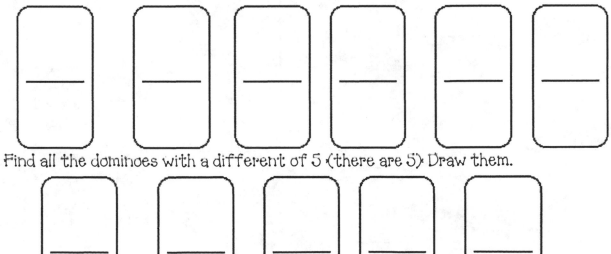

Domino Match-up
(continued)

Find all the dominoes with a different of 6 (there are 4) Draw them.

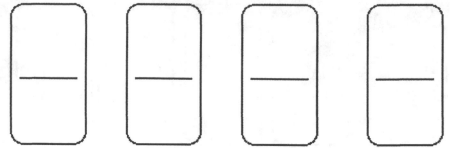

Find all the dominoes with a different of 7 (there are 3) Draw them.

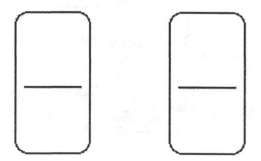

Find all the dominoes with a different of 8 (there are 2) Draw them.

Find all the dominoes with a different of 9 (there is 1) Draw it.

Congratulations!   You did it!

Name_____ Date_____

Subtraction Activities for facts with Minuends to 18

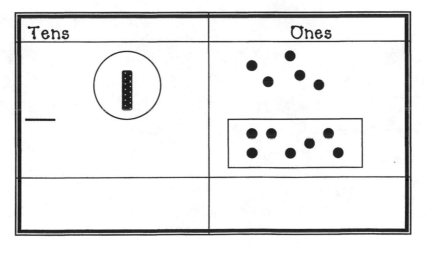

SUBTRACTION CONCEPT:
Developing basic subtraction facts with minuends to 18

Basic Facts and Beans

Preparation:
- Distribute a **Subtraction Mat** (page 111) to each student. Copy one mat onto an overhead transparency for demonstration purposes. Using a red and green overhead marker, color the circles green and the squares red.

- Duplicate the **Bean It Beanery** for each student (page 112).

- Supply each student with 20 small red beans and 1 beanstick kit (page 52)

- Students will need a red and green crayon.

Procedure:
- Before students begin the activity have them color the circles green and the squares red on their subtraction mats (page 111).

- Use the overhead transparency of page 111 with beansticks and beans to illustrate several subtraction problems.
Example dialogue:
"Let's set up the subtraction problem 16-7 on our subtraction mats.

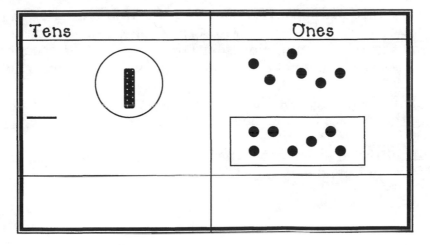

How much do we owe? **7**
Do we have enough? **No**
Take a ten. What's that ten going to look like? **7 + 3** *(debt + what's left)*
Pay debts. (Take off 7 with 7)
What's left? **9**

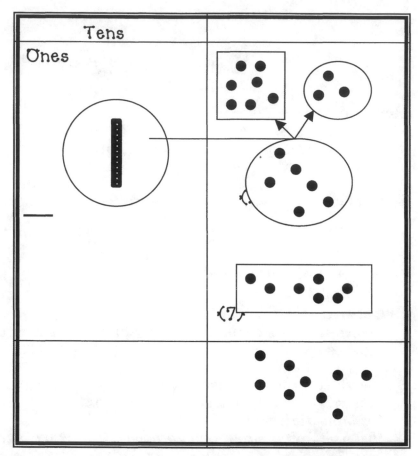

- Repeat the procedure with a variety of problems reinforcing the thought process over and over again. At this stage it will seem so much easier just to have the students memorize all the minuends to 18 but they allow the student to practice the thought process which will be valuable as the skill level progresses

- Use page 112 for additional practice. Encourage students to work with their beans, saying the process in their heads and recording the answers.

- Students will get to the place where they can mentally look at the debt and add what's left to the minuend very quickly.

Subtraction Mat

Tens	Ones

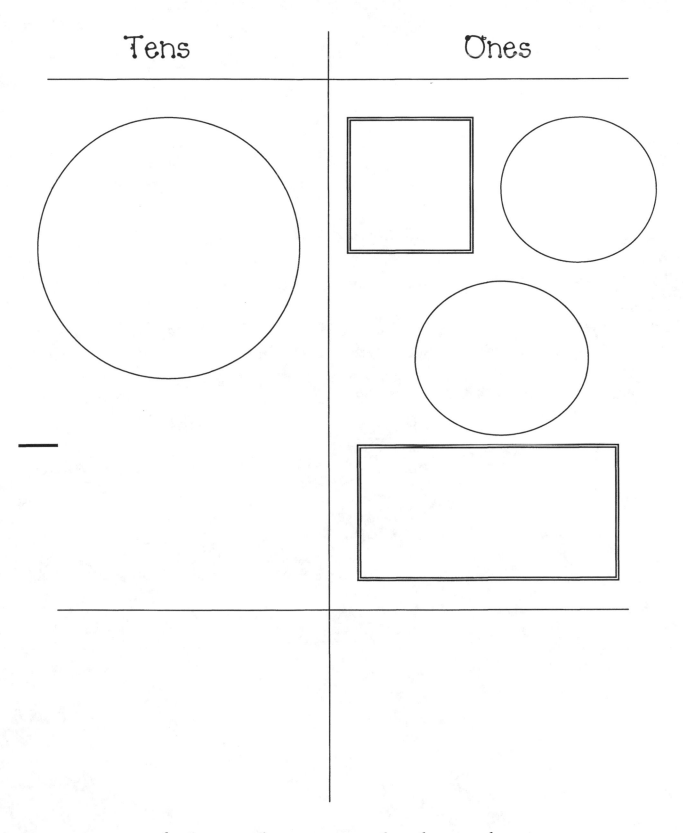

Bean It Beanery

Use your beans and subtraction mat to solve and record these problems.

1. 10-4=	2. 15-7=	3. 17-9=
4. 17-8=	5. 11-4=	6. 13-9=
7. 13-8=	8. 15-6=	9. 12-1=
10. 15-8=	11. 12-5=	12. 17-6=
13. 14-5=	14. 11-3=	15. 16-9=
16. 12-4=	17. 18-9=	18. 18-2=
19. 11-5=	20. 17-7=	21. 11-6=
22. 10-8=	23. 16-7=	24. 12-3=
25. 16-8=	26. 10-2=	27. 14-6=
28. 13-7=	29. 11-7=	30. 13-5=
31. 18-3=	32. 13-6=	33. 12-2=
34. 10-3=	35. 10-7=	36. 15-9=
37. 14-8=	38. 12-6=	39. 18-5=
40. 16-3=	41. 14-9=	42. 10-6=
43. 18-4=	44. 16-2=	45. 11-2=
46. 14-7=	47. 12-8=	48. 13-4=
49. 11-1=	50. 15-3=	51. 14-2=
52. 16-4=	53. 17-5=	54. 12-9=
55. 9-6=	56. 18-7=	57. 18-6=
58. 12-7=	59. 11-8=	60. 8-5=
61. 9-7=	62. 10-9=	63. 7-4=
64. 11-9=	65. 10-5=	66. 18-9=

SUBTRACTION CONCEPT:
Practicing basic subtration facts with minuends to 18

Domino Hunt

Preparation:
- Provide each student with a Double-Nine domino set (page 6,22)
- Duplicate the **Domino Hunt** workmats on pages 114-118 for each student.
- Create an overhead transparency of the workmats and dominoes to use for whole class demonstration.

Procedure:
- Illustrate with the overhead dominoes how to read a domino as part of the subtraction problem.

    Example:

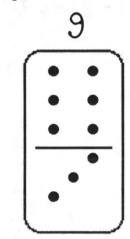 **This reads**

9-6=3

- Continue to reinforce the "thinking process":
    - *What do I owe?* **6**
    - *Do I have enough?* **Yes**
    - *Pay debt.*
    - *What's left?* **3**
- The workmats on pages 114-118 to provide lots of practice.

Extra Challenge : Students take a set of dominoes and write subtraction sentences with all of them.

Domino Hunt A

Hunt for dominoes to solve the following subtraction problems. You may not use a domino more than once.

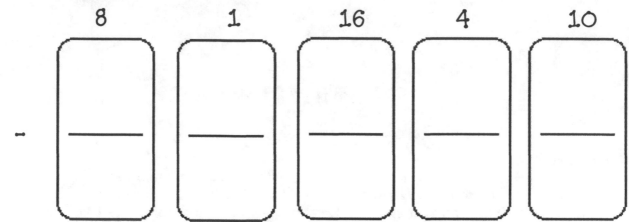

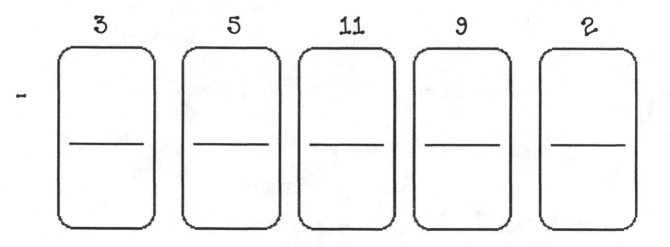

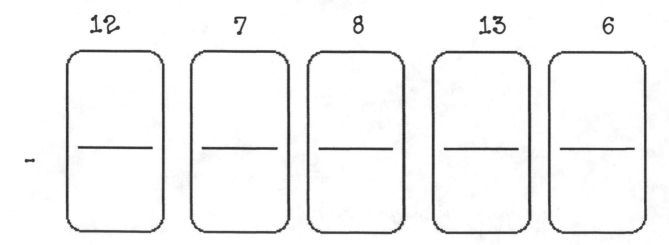

Domino Hunt B

Hunt for dominoes to solve the following subtraction problems. You may not use a domino more than once.

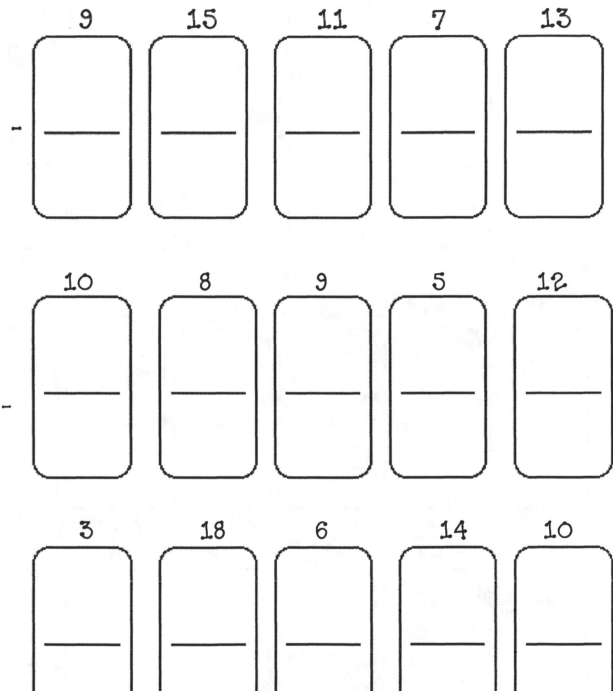

Super Domino Hunt – Part 1

Hunt for dominoes to solve all the subtraction problems. You will need Part 2&3 in addition to this sheet. You may only use each domino once. Good luck!

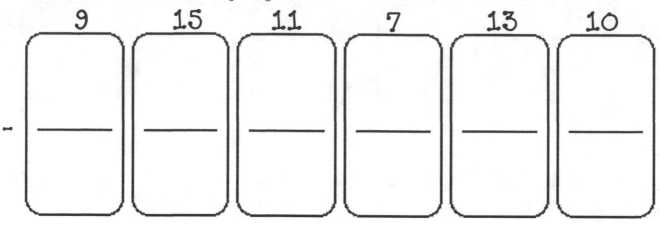

| 9 | 15 | 11 | 7 | 13 | 10 |

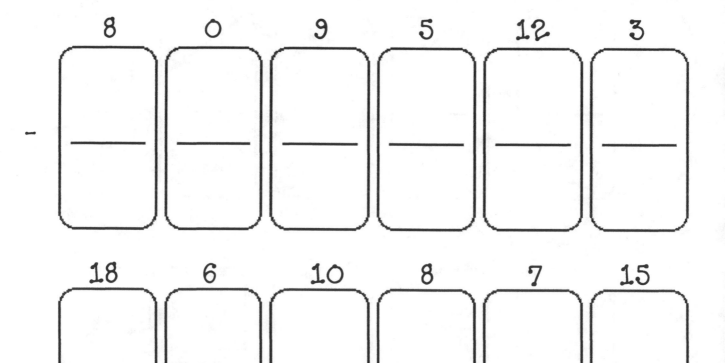

| 8 | 0 | 9 | 5 | 12 | 3 |

| 18 | 6 | 10 | 8 | 7 | 15 |

Super Domino Hunt – Part 2

Hunt for dominoes to solve all the subtraction problems. You will need Part 1 & 3 in addition to this sheet. You may only use each domino once. Good luck!

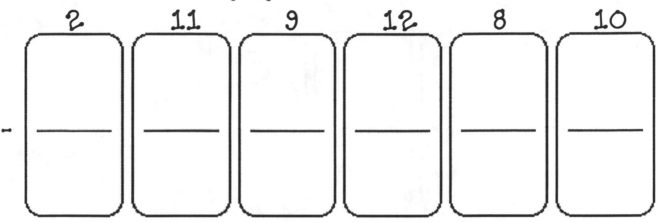

2	11	9	12	8	10

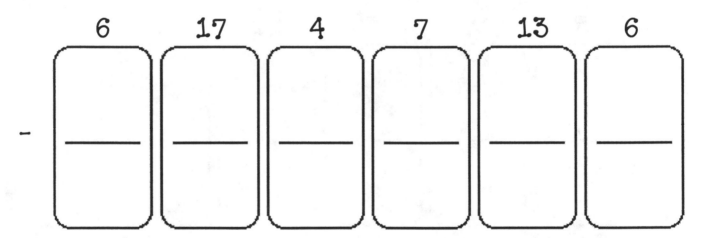

6	17	4	7	13	6

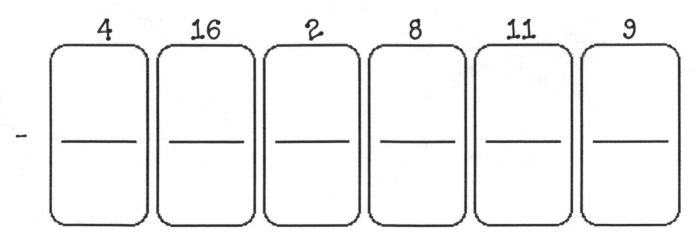

4	16	2	8	11	9

Super Domino Hunt – Part 3

Hunt for dominoes to solve all the subtraction problems. You will need Part 1 & 3 in addition to this sheet. You may only use each domino once. Good luck!

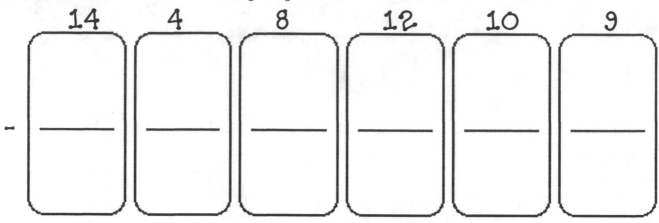

| 14 | 4 | 8 | 12 | 10 | 9 |

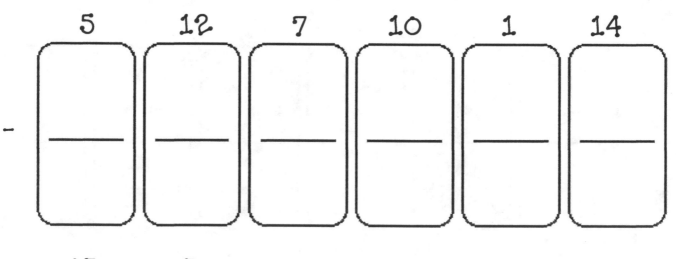

| 5 | 12 | 7 | 10 | 1 | 14 |

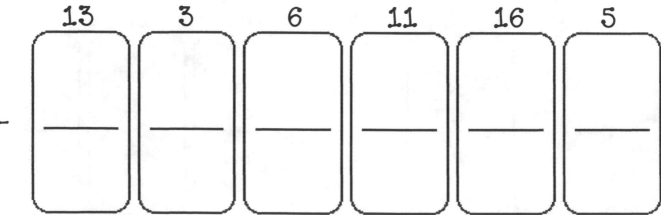

| 13 | 3 | 6 | 11 | 16 | 5 |

SUBTRACTION CONCEPT:
Practicing basic subtraction facts with minuends to 18.

Subtract as you Go

Preparation:
- Provide each group of two students a **Subtract as you Go** game mat (page 120.

- Write the numerals 0-9 on two sets of index cards (per group of two students)

- Supply each student with a game marker different from their partners.

Procedure:
- Game markers are placed on the **Subtract as you Go** gameboard in the "start" square.

- Please the numeral cards face down in the center of the playing area.

- On each turn, a player draws a card and subtracts that number from the first number on the game mat. If the card drawn is larger than the number on the board, the player cannot move. Players need to verbalize the following on each turn:

  What they have
  What they owe
  How much is left

- For each correct answer, player moves game marker the number of spaces left from the problem in the direction of the game mat arrows.

Example of play

$$\begin{array}{c} 9 \end{array}$$

Player moves marker 8 spaces

2	6	5	3	7	End
12	7	9	8	4	9
8	14	12	11	6	16
17	12	11	13	18	14
ST	18	15	8	10	4

$$\begin{array}{r} 17 \\ -\ 9 \\ \hline 8 \end{array}$$

Subtract as you Go

2 →	6	5	3	7 →	End

2 → 6	5	3	7 → End
12 ← 7	9	8	4 ← 9
8 → 14	12	11	6 → 16
12 5	7	9	5 13
14 → 11	10	17	15 → 3
9 ← 6	18	11	7 ← 15
17 → 12	11	13	18 → 14
12 ← 16	17	6	15 ← 13
Start → 18	15	8	10 → 4

120

SUBTRACTION CONCEPT:
Reinforcing the basic subtraction facts with minuends to 18.

Sub War

Preparation:
- Copy pages 122-128 onto cardstock. Cut out the set to make a deck of cards.
- Each group of 2,4 or 6 students will need two complete decks.

Procedure:
- The shuffled deck of **Sub War** cards is dealt evenly to each player in a group of 2, 4, or 6 students.

- Placing the cards face down, each player turns over their top card.

- Each player reads their card aloud, identifies the debt, and tells the rest of the players what is left.
  > *Example:* **16-8** *Sixteen minus eight. The debt is 8 and 8 is left.*
- The player with the highest difference takes all the top cards and places them in their own individual pile.

- If a tie (war) occurs, each player involved turns over their next top card and the highest difference takes all the top cards.

- The player that ends up with the most card in their pile is the winner.

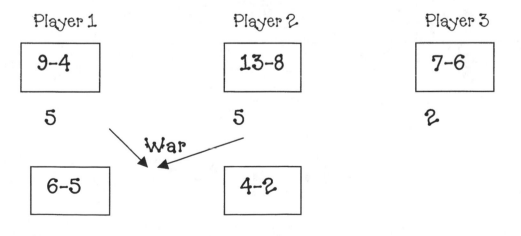

Player 2 takes all 5 cards

Sub War Cards

Sub War!	Sub War!	Sub War!	Sub War!
10-9	10-8	10-7	10-6

Sub War!	Sub War!	Sub War!	Sub War!
10-5	10-4	10-3	10-2

Sub War!	Sub War!	Sub War!	Sub War!
10-1	10-0	9-9	9-8

Sub War!	Sub War!	Sub War!	Sub War!
9-7	9-6	9-5	9-4

Sub War Cards

Sub War!	Sub War!	Sub War!	Sub War!
9-3	9-2	9-1	9-0
Sub War!	Sub War!	Sub War!	Sub War!
8-8	8-7	8-6	8-5
Sub War!	Sub War!	Sub War!	Sub War!
8-4	8-3	8-2	8-1
Sub War!	Sub War!	Sub War!	Sub War!
8-0	7-7	7-6	7-5

Sub War Cards

Sub War! 7-4	Sub War! 7-3	Sub War! 7-2	Sub War! 7-1
Sub War! 7-0	Sub War! 6-6	Sub War! 6-5	Sub War! 6-4
Sub War! 6-3	Sub War! 6-2	Sub War! 6-1	Sub War! 6-0
Sub War! 5-5	Sub War! 5-4	Sub War! 5-3	Sub War! 5-2

Sub War Cards ✏️

Sub War!	Sub War!	Sub War!	Sub War!
5-1	5-0	4-4	4-3
Sub War!	Sub War!	Sub War!	Sub War!
4-2	4-1	4-0	3-3
Sub War!	Sub War!	Sub War!	Sub War!
3-2	3-1	3-0	2-2
Sub War!	Sub War!	Sub War!	Sub War!
2-1	2-0	1-1	1-0

Sub War Cards

Sub War! 11-9	Sub War! 11-8	Sub War! 11-7	Sub War! 11-6
Sub War! 11-5	Sub War! 11-4	Sub War! 11-3	Sub War! 11-2
Sub War! 12-9	Sub War! 12-8	Sub War! 12-7	Sub War! 12-6
Sub War! 12-5	Sub War! 12-4	Sub War! 13-9	Sub War! 13-8

Sub War Cards

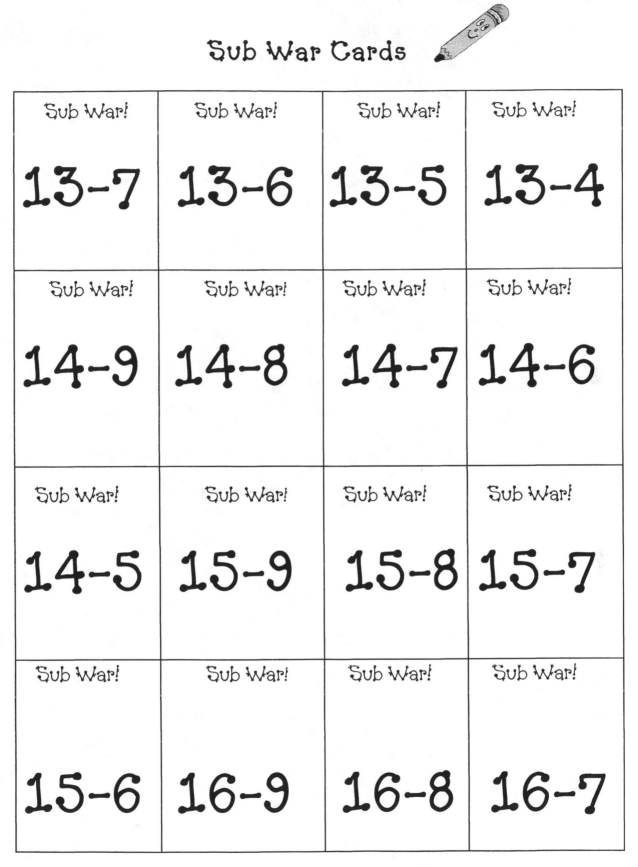

Sub War!	Sub War!	Sub War!	Sub War!
13-7	13-6	13-5	13-4
Sub War!	Sub War!	Sub War!	Sub War!
14-9	14-8	14-7	14-6
Sub War!	Sub War!	Sub War!	Sub War!
14-5	15-9	15-8	15-7
Sub War!	Sub War!	Sub War!	Sub War!
15-6	16-9	16-8	16-7

Sub War Cards

Sub War!	Sub War!	Sub War!	Sub War!
17-9	**17-8**	**17-7**	**17-6**
Sub War!	Sub War!	Sub War!	Sub War!
Sub War!	Sub War!	Sub War!	Sub War!
Sub War!	Sub War!	Sub War!	Sub War!

Activities For Multi-Digit Subtraction

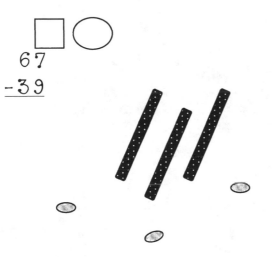

```
    □  ○
  6 7
- 3 9
```

Ones
What do I owe? 8
Do I have enough? No
Take a ten (8+2)
Pay Debt
What's left ? 4
Tens
What do I owe? 1
Do I have enough? Yes
Pay dcbt
What's left? 3

SUBTRACTION CONCEPT:
Developing Multi-digit subtraction with and without regrouping

Subtract Those Beans

Preparation:
- Construct **Subtraction Trading Boards** for each student (see instructions on page 134. A reversible trading board can be constructed by drawing this on the back of the addition trading boards constructed from page 51.

- Distribute beanstick kits to each student. See page 52-53 for materials and construction instructions.

- Make an overhead transparency of the **Subtraction Trading Board** and overhead beansticks to use for illustration purposes

  Special Note: You may use base ten blocks instead of beansticks. Base ten blocks are more appropriate for 5-8th graders.

Procedure:
1. Using the overhead projector, explain the various features of the subtraction trading board, i.e., "debt" boxes and "what's left" circles.

2. Remind students that beans are only removed from debt boxes when the debt is paid.

3. Model the thinking and manipulative process of subtraction with problems that require no regrouping and regrouping. See pages 79-82 for subtraction information.

(continued on page 132)

Example with no regrouping:

"Set up 325-14 on your subtraction trading boards."

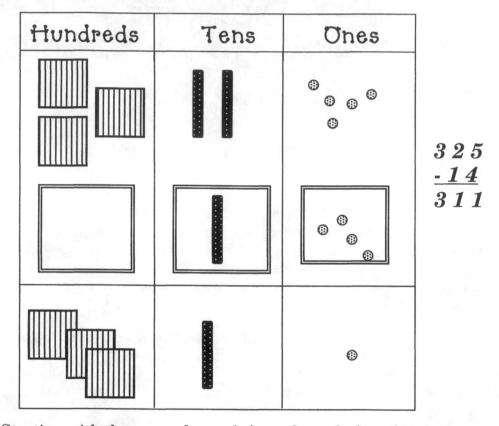

$$\begin{array}{r} 3\ 2\ 5 \\ -\ 1\ 4 \\ \hline 3\ 1\ 1 \end{array}$$

Starting with the ones column, let's go through the subtraction process.
What is the first question we ask? **What do I owe? 4**
Do we have enough? Yes
Pay debt. Remove 4 from what you have and the 4 from the debt box
    as a reminder that you paid it.
What's left? 1 Bring the 1 down into the answer column.
Now let's look at the tens column.
What do we owe? 1
Pay debt. Remove 1 from what you have and the 1 from the debt box
    as a reminder that the debt is paid.
Now move to the hundreds column.
What do we owe? Nothing Bring down the 3 into the answer
column.

Example dialogue with regrouping:
Set up 453-47 on your subtraction trading boards.
(Note: illustration shows the complete problem)

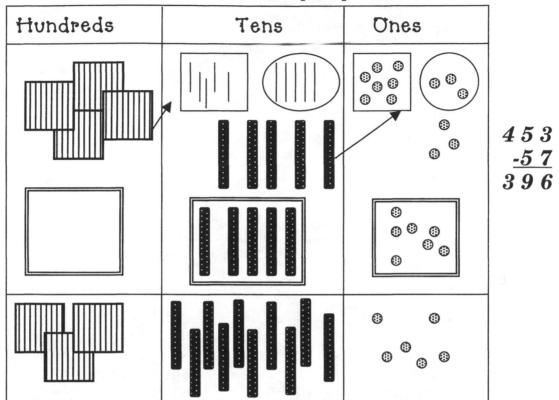

Hundreds	Tens	Ones

$$
\begin{array}{r}
4\ 5\ 3 \\
-5\ 7 \\
\hline
3\ 9\ 6
\end{array}
$$

Starting with the ones column, let's go through the subtraction process.

What do we owe? 7

Do we have enough? No

Take a ten. Take a beanstick (1 ten) from the tens column and trade it for the debt (7) plus what is left to make ten (3)

Pay debt. Remove 7 from what you have and the 7 from the debt box as a reminder that you paid it.

What is left? 6 Bring that 6 down into the answer column

Now move to the tens column

What do we owe? 5

Do we have enough? No

Take a ten. Take a beanstick (1 ten) from the tens column and trade it for the debt (5) plus what is left to make ten (5)

Pay debt. Remove 5 from what you have and the 5 from the debt box.

What is left? 9 Bring the 9 down into the answer column.

Now move to the hundreds column

What do we owe? Nothing

Bring down the 3 into the answer column.

Students can use the subtraction trading board to practice a variety of problems. Page 135 includes more practice problems.

Subtraction Trading Board
Instructions for construction

Materials Needed:
- 45cm x 60cm white posterboard (1 per student)
- black, red, and green permanent markers
- ruler

Construction:
Design the board according to the pattern below:

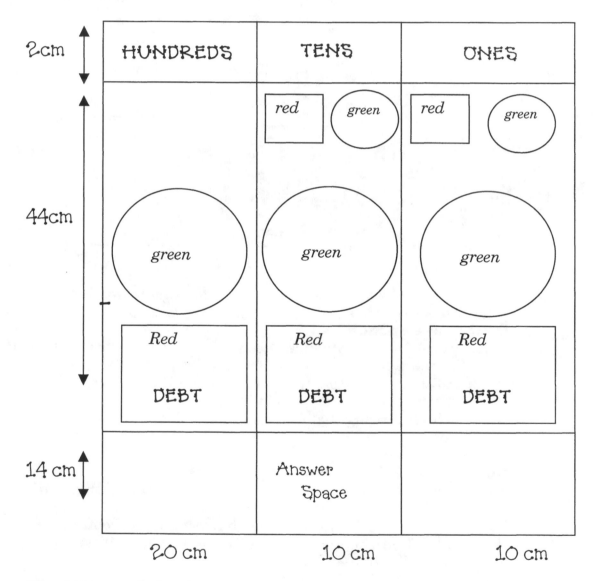

Special note: *Before laminating this, you may want to use the other side for the addition trading board (page 51)*

Subtraction Bean It

Use your beansticks and subtraction trading board to show and solve these addition problems.

1. 123
    - 54

2. 346
    - 107

3. 26
    - 15

4. 691
    - 123

5. 46
    - 17

6. 233
    - 125

7. 144
    - 72

8. 672
    - 428

9. 159
    - 87

10. 397
    - 85

11. 222
    - 62

12. 359
    - 35

13. 777
    - 397

14. 997
    - 652

15. 215
    - 137

16. 500
    - 32

17. 452
    - 251

18. 971
    - 76

Name_____ Date_____

SUBTRACTION CONCEPT:
Developing multi-digit addition using representational notation

Draw those beans

Preparation:
- Provide each student with a subtraction trading board (page 134) and a beanstick set (page 52-53).

- Duplicate pages 137-138 to each student.

- Use the overhead manipulatives created in **Add Those Beans** (page 49) and make overhead transparencies of pages 137-138.

Procedure:
1. Using the overhead manipulatives, illustrate several subtraction problems as you did in the **Basic Facts and Beans** lesson on pages 109-110.

2. Instruct students to use the following system of notation that corresponds with the manipulatives:

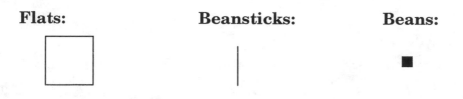

Flats: **Beansticks:**   **Beans:**

3. Distribute **Draw Those Beans** practice sheet (page 137) and illustrate with the overhead transparencies and manipulatives the first two problems. Let students complete the practice sheet to develop fluency with the notation system.

4. Use **Draw Those Beans** workmat (page 138) for extra practice or use any subtraction problems from textbooks or other sources.

> *Special Note:* Students can also use real beans on their trading boards and then then draw the notations on to the worksheets.

Draw those beans

1.

Hundreds	Tens	Ones
5	4	3
–		
[ ]	7	6

2.

Hundreds	Tens	Ones
3	5	0
–		
[ ]	6	5

3.

Hundreds	Tens	Ones
6	8	4
–		
[ ]	8	8

4.

Hundreds	Tens	Ones
5	2	5
–		
[ ]	4	7

5.

Hundreds	Tens	Ones
7	3	2
–		
[ ]	6	7

6.

Hundreds	Tens	Ones
8	5	2
–		
4	9	6
[ ]	[ ]	[ ]

Draw those beans

Workmat

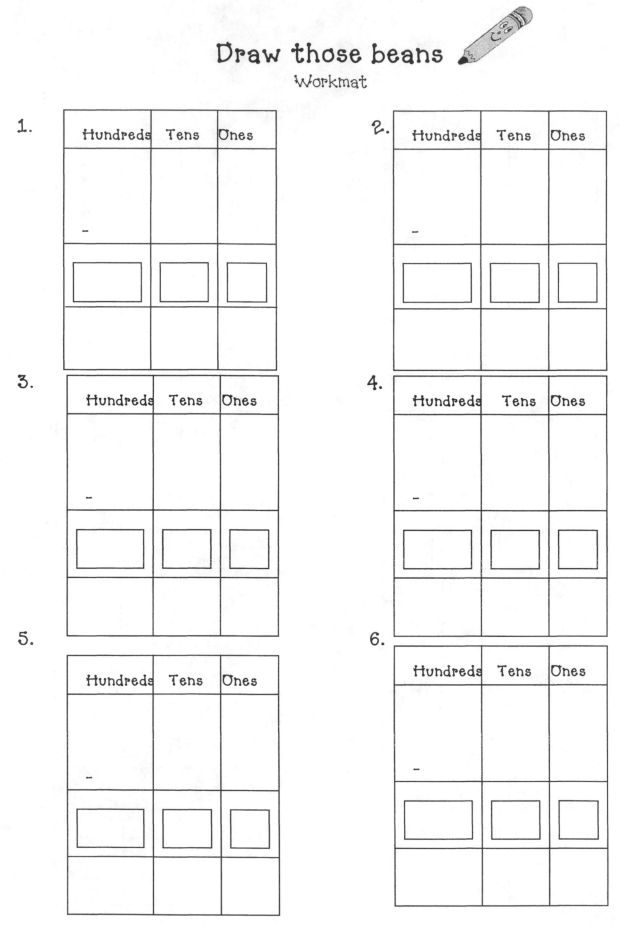

![apple core] SUBTRACTION CONCEPT:
Developing multi-digit subtraction Without those beans!

No Beans Please

Preparation:
- Provide each student with a copy of the worksheet on page 140-141.

Procedure:
- Students solve multi-digit subtraction problems and record their work with the representational notation learned on page 136.

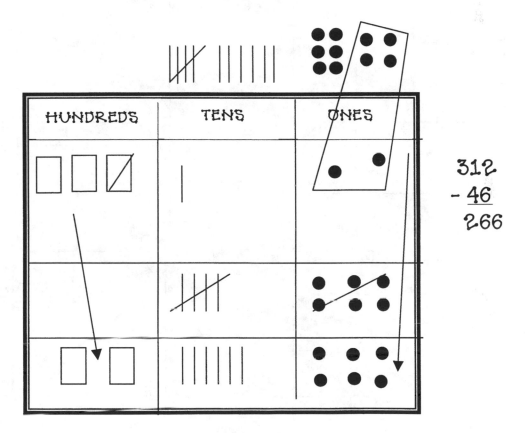

- If students experience problems using the notation without the beans, let them validate their answers with the beans.

No Beans Please!

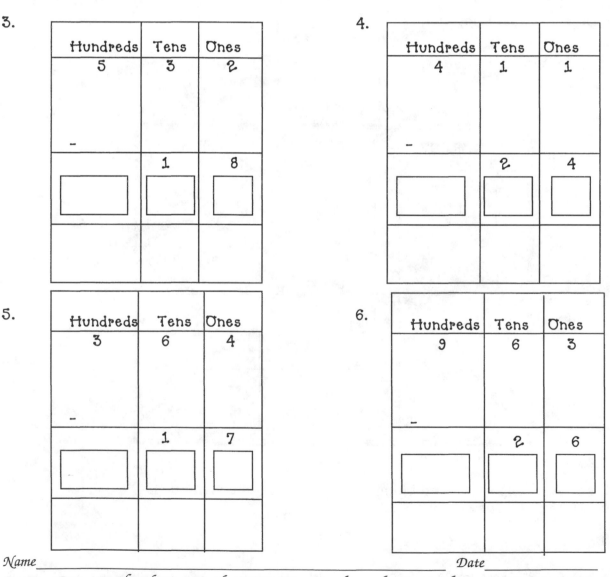

1.

Hundreds	Tens	Ones
3	1	2
-		
	4	6

2.

Hundreds	Tens	Ones
6	4	5
-		
	7	

3.

Hundreds	Tens	Ones
5	3	2
-		
	1	8

4.

Hundreds	Tens	Ones
4	1	1
-		
	2	4

5.

Hundreds	Tens	Ones
3	6	4
-		
	1	7

6.

Hundreds	Tens	Ones
9	6	3
-		
	2	6

Name_____ Date_____

No Beans Please

1.

Hundreds	Tens	Ones
3	2	0
-		
	3	5

2.

Hundreds	Tens	Ones
7	6	0
-		
	2	8

3.

Hundreds	Tens	Ones
4	1	1
-		
	2	4

4.

Hundreds	Tens	Ones
8	1	7
-		
	4	2

5.

Hundreds	Tens	Ones
3	4	0
-		
	6	8

6.

Hundreds	Tens	Ones
6	2	4
-		
	5	6

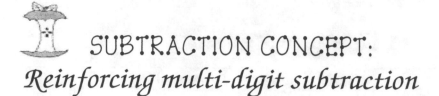

SUBTRACTION CONCEPT:
Reinforcing multi-digit subtraction

Think and Subtract

Preparation:
- Duplicate pages 143-146 as appropriate for student skill level.

Procedure:
- The worksheets (pages 143-146) are designed to accommodate the subtraction thinking process. Use them as needed to reinforce multi-digit subtraction.

- The worksheets progress sequentially from easy to hard. Students can always use their subtraction trading boards (page 134) and beans if needed. Usually by this stage of the process they are not necessary.

Example:

$$\begin{array}{r} 5\,2 \\ -\ 1\,8 \\ \hline 3\,4 \end{array}$$

> **Ones**
> **What do I owe? 8**
> **Do I have enough? No**
> **Take a ten (8+2)**
> **Pay Debt**
> **What's left ? 4**
>
> **Tens**
> **What do I owe? 1**
> **Do I have enough? Yes**
> **Pay debt**
> **What's left? 3**

Think & Subtract A

Draw red boxes around your debts first. Think through each step as you subtract.

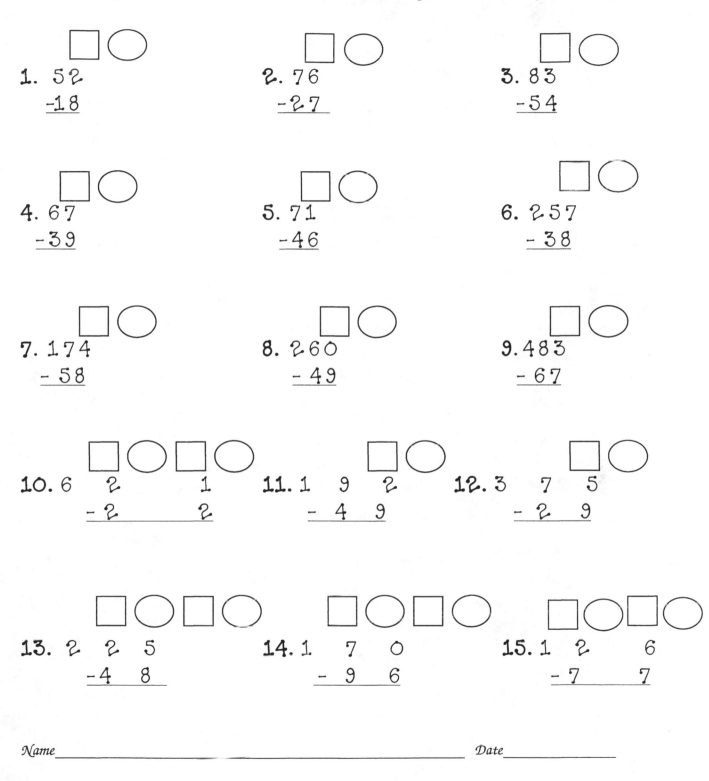

1. 52
   -18

2. 76
   -27

3. 83
   -54

4. 67
   -39

5. 71
   -46

6. 257
   - 38

7. 174
   - 58

8. 260
   - 49

9. 483
   - 67

10. 6 2   1
     -2   2

11. 1 9 2
       - 4 9

12. 3 7 5
      - 2 9

13. 2 2 5
      -4 8

14. 1 7 0
        - 9 6

15. 1 2   6
       - 7   7

Name_____ Date_____

Think & Subtract B

Draw red boxes around your debts first. Think through each step as you subtract.

$\square \bigcirc$

$$
\begin{array}{r}
1. \quad 7\ 1 \\
-\underline{4\ 8}
\end{array}
\qquad
\begin{array}{r}
2. \quad 4\ 2 \\
-\underline{1\ 6}
\end{array}
\qquad
\begin{array}{r}
3. \quad 1\ 3\ 6 \\
-\underline{\ \ 2\ 7}
\end{array}
$$

$$
\begin{array}{r}
4. \quad 3\ 5\ 2 \\
-\underline{\ \ 2\ 7}
\end{array}
\qquad
\begin{array}{r}
5. \quad 2\ 1\ 7 \\
-\underline{\ 4\ 3}
\end{array}
\qquad
\begin{array}{r}
6. \quad 7\ 2\ 4 \\
-\underline{\ 3\ 5}
\end{array}
$$

$$
\begin{array}{r}
7. \quad 4\ 6\ 2 \\
-\underline{\ 8\ 4}
\end{array}
\qquad
\begin{array}{r}
8. \quad 8\ 5\ 4 \\
-\underline{\ 7\ 8}
\end{array}
\qquad
\begin{array}{r}
9. \quad 6\ 3\ 4 \\
-\underline{\ 7\ 6}
\end{array}
$$

$$
\begin{array}{r}
10. \quad 3\ 1\ 2 \\
-\underline{\ 4\ 5}
\end{array}
\qquad
\begin{array}{r}
11. \quad 2\ 2\ 6 \\
-\underline{\ 5\ 8}
\end{array}
\qquad
\begin{array}{r}
12. \quad 8\ 4\ 3 \\
-\underline{\ \ 8\ 6}
\end{array}
$$

$$
\begin{array}{r}
13. \quad 4\ 7\ 2 \\
-\underline{\ 8\ 9}
\end{array}
\qquad
\begin{array}{r}
14. \quad 9\ 7\ 1 \\
-\underline{\ 9\ 6}
\end{array}
$$

Name_____ Date_____

Think & Subtract C

Draw red boxes around your debts first. Think through each step as you subtract.

☐○☐○   ☐○☐○   ☐○☐○

1. 4 3   2   2. 6 2   4   3. 3 6   2
  −   4   8   −   5   6   −   2 7   3

4. 5 2 5   5. 7 2 5   6. 7 3 8
  −   4 7   −   5 2 8   −   3 9

7. 6 4 3   8. 9 4 5   9. 4 1 6
  − 5 6 5   − 1 6 7   − 1 5 8

10. 7 6 3   11. 9 8 1   12. 6 4 5
   − 6 7 7   −   8 5   − 4 9 7

Name_____   Date_____

Think & Subtract D

Draw red boxes around your debts first. Think through each step as you subtract.

1. $\begin{array}{r} 3,842 \\ -936 \\ \hline \end{array}$

2. $\begin{array}{r} 4,632 \\ -804 \\ \hline \end{array}$

3. $\begin{array}{r} 6,275 \\ -793 \\ \hline \end{array}$

4. $\begin{array}{r} 5,635 \\ -537 \\ \hline \end{array}$

5. $\begin{array}{r} 2,153 \\ -448 \\ \hline \end{array}$

6. $\begin{array}{r} 5,678 \\ -2,389 \\ \hline \end{array}$

7. $\begin{array}{r} 4,356 \\ -1,584 \\ \hline \end{array}$

8. $\begin{array}{r} 7,216 \\ -3,722 \\ \hline \end{array}$

9. $\begin{array}{r} 9,651 \\ -2,372 \\ \hline \end{array}$

Name_____ Date_____

SUBTRACTION CONCEPT:
Developing multi-digit subtraction with zeros in the minuend

Sub Zeros

Preparation:
- Supply each student with a copy of the *sub Zero* worksheet on page 148.

Procedure:
1. Review the subtraction thought process (see pages 80-82). Study the example below. It is helpful to use graph paper to keep the columns lined up.

Example:

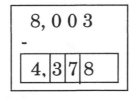

2. Draw a box around debts. Starting with the ones column....
   What do I owe? 8
   Do I have enough? No
   Take a ten. Notice the tens column does not have any to take. Go to the next column (hundreds). Opps...none there either. Go to the next column (thousands). Plenty there!

3. Now go back the way you came – don't get lost! As you travel to each column, give what is needed (debt + left over to equal ten). Only take from the leftovers to give to the column to the right.

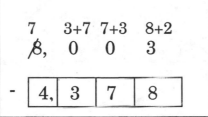

4. Here comes the fun part!!!
   Pay the debts! Cross off each debt as paid and bring down what is left.

```
     7    3+7  7+3   8+2
     8,   0    0     3
     4,   3    7     8
     ─────────────────────
     3,   6    2     5
```

This process becomes very easy with just a little practice. Very large problems can be solved quickly and accurately. Students actually enjoy subtraction again!

Sub Zeros

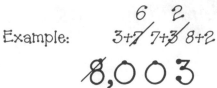

Example:

$$\begin{array}{r} 6 \quad 2 \\ 3{+}7 \;\; 7{+}3 \;\; 8{+}2 \\ 8,003 \\ -4,378 \\ \hline \end{array}$$

$$\begin{array}{r} 3{+}7 \;\; 7{+}3 \;\; 8{+}2 \\ 8,003 \\ -4,378 \\ \hline 3,625 \end{array}$$

What do I owe?   Do I have enough?   take tens   Pay debts
You did it!

1. $\begin{array}{r} 6,003 \\ -2,346 \\ \hline \end{array}$

2. $\begin{array}{r} 7,005 \\ -3,268 \\ \hline \end{array}$

3. $\begin{array}{r} 9,004 \\ -4,976 \\ \hline \end{array}$

4. $\begin{array}{r} 1,900 \\ -1,858 \\ \hline \end{array}$

5. $\begin{array}{r} 500 \\ -\;\;43 \\ \hline \end{array}$

6. $\begin{array}{r} 1,007 \\ -\;983 \\ \hline \end{array}$

7. $\begin{array}{r} 6,700 \\ -5,279 \\ \hline \end{array}$

8. $\begin{array}{r} 2,600 \\ -\;\;344 \\ \hline \end{array}$

9. $\begin{array}{r} 5,801 \\ -3,622 \\ \hline \end{array}$

If you used graph paper to help you, staple it to this worksheet.

Name_____ Date_____

SUBTRACTION CONCEPT:
Practicing multi-digit subtraction with dominoes

Double Domino It

Preparation:
- Supply each student with a Double-Six set of dominoes (page 6).
- Duplicate the **Double Domino It** worksheet on page 150 for each student.

Procedure:
- Students will use their dominoes to create subtraction problems that all equal the same difference

- The difference may be chosen by the student. Encourage them to choose a number between 7-53.

- The following differences do not require regrouping:
  10,11,12,13,14,15,16,20,21,22,23,24,25,30,31,33,324,35,40,41,42,43,44,50,51,52 53.
  -
- The following differences do require regrouping:
  7,8,9,17,18,26,27,28,29,36,37,38,39,46,47,48,49

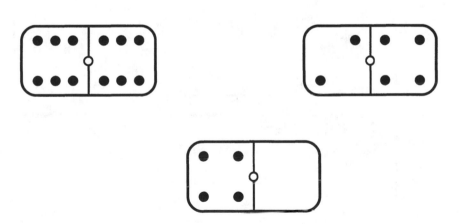

Double Domino It

Use your dominoes to create as many problems as possible with the difference of _____

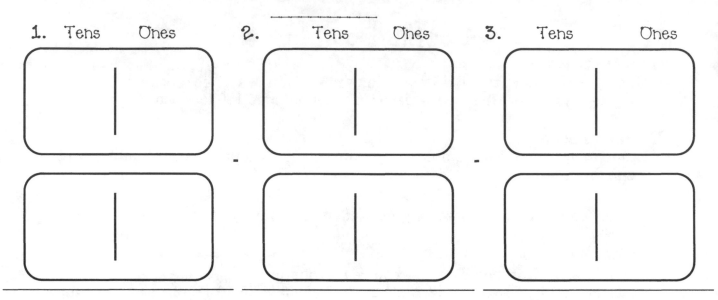

1. Tens   Ones

2. Tens   Ones

3. Tens   Ones

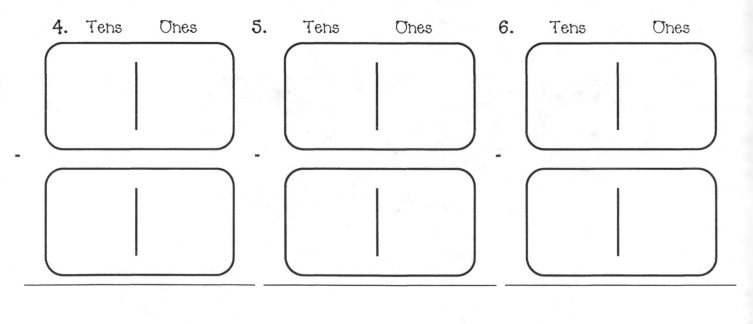

4. Tens   Ones

5. Tens   Ones

6. Tens   Ones

Name_____   Date_____

Activities for Addition and Subtraction

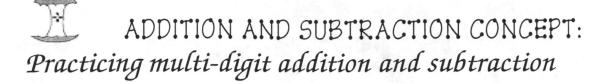

Magic 1,089

Preparation:
- Make a copy of page 154 for each student.

Procedure:
- Magic 1,089 is a fun way to reinforce addition and subtraction. Introduce the activity by informing students that they are going to learn a special formula to be used with addition and subtraction that will enable them to always get the same answer : 1,089 (except if they make a mistake of course!).

Follow these special formula steps:

1. Start with any 3 digit numeral (make sure the first digit is larger than the last digit. *Example:* **421**

2. Subtract the opposite of the 3 digit numeral

$$\begin{array}{r} 421 \\ -124 \\ \hline 297 \end{array}$$

3. Add the opposite of that answer

$$\begin{array}{r} 421 \\ -124 \\ \hline 297 \\ +792 \\ \hline 1{,}089 \end{array}$$

4. If 1,089 is not reached after step 3, repeat steps 1-3 until 1,089 becomes the final answer.

Special Note: If a 2 digit numeral is used, the answer will be 99. Have students explore what answers 4,5, or 6 digits will produce.

Magic 1,089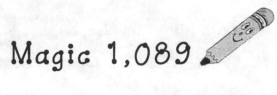

Use the special 1,089 formula to solve the following problems.

1. 391

2. 984

3. 824

4. 837

5. 766

6. 543

7. 641

8. 532

Name_____ Date_____

ADDITION AND SUBTRACTION CONCEPT:
Practicing multi-digit addition and subtraction

Preparation:
- Provide each student with a set of 0-9 tiles.
  - ➢ Tiles can be made from small one-inch bathroom tiles. Write the numerals 0-9 with a permanent marker. Use different colors to distinguish sets.
  - ➢ Tiles are also available from school supply stores.
  - ➢ A tile pattern is provided on page 156. Copy the pattern onto cardstock and laminate.
- Supply each student with graph paper.

Procedure:
- Divide students into groups of 2-10 players.

Rules of the game:

1. Tile sets are placed face down like scrabble pieces in the center of the playing area. Each player turns over a tile. The player with the highest tile is the dealer.

2. The dealer decides how many squares will be marked off on the graph paper for the game. For example, if the dealer wants four-digit numerals to be used, they call out "four" and each player marks their graph paper as shown:

3. The dealer decides whether the game will be addition or subtraction by calling out "add 'em" or "subtract 'em."

4. Tiles are mixed up by the dealer and one if turned over. Players place that number in any empty space in their graph square. Players need to use a strategy so that the problem can be solved (especially for subtraction). Dealer continues to turn up one tile at a time until the graph square is filled by the players.

5. Players add or subtract, depending on what was called. The player with the largest answer scores ten points.

6. Game continues until one player reaches 100 points.

Numeral Tiles

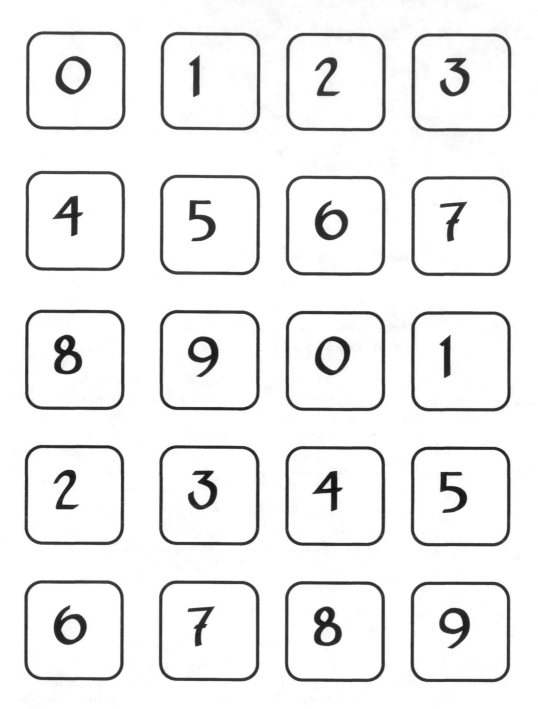

Answer Keys

Page 8
Row 1 – 6,2,5,5,6,5
Row 2 – 6,1,3,3,5,3
Row 3 – 2,2,2,4,6,4

Page 13
1. 8+5=13
2. 9+7=16
3. 7+8=15
4. 9+5=14
5. 8+10=18
6. 6+7=13

Page 14
1) 15 2) 8 3) 6 4) 13 5) 11 6) 9

Page 15
1) 15 2) 12 3) 14 4) 12 5) 17 6) 12

Page 54
1) 63 2) 117 3) 113 4) 117 5) 56 6)85 7) 58 8) 77 9) 43 10) 84
11) 61 12) 63 13) 75 14) 69 15) 109 16) 155 17) 139 18) 199 19) 201
20) 233 21) 196

Page 56
1) 72 2) 374 3) 93 4) 103 5) 57 6) 204

Page 68
1) 14 2) 19 3) 17 4) 12 5) 13 6) 17

Page 70
1) 15 2) 13 3) 17 4) 16 5) 15 6) 17

Page 72
1) 12 2) 19 3) 13 4) 14 5) 14 6) 16

Page 74

Page 76

1) 5,221 2) 7,878 3) 4,199 4) 10,235 5) 61,455 6) 37,626 7) 102,235
8) 1,159,813 9) 1,302,570 10) 602,389 11) 47,474,942 12) 777,554
Bonus: 4,700.124.193

Page 112

1)6 2)8 3)8 4)7 5)7 6)4 7)5 8)9 9)11 10)7 11)7 12)11 13)9 14)8
15)7 16)8 17)9 18)16 19)6 20)10 21)5 22)2 23)9 24)9 25)8 26)8
27)8 28)6 29)4 30)8 31)15 32)7 3310 34)7 35)3 36)6 37)6 38)6
39)13 40)13 41)5 42)4 43)14 44)14 45)9 46)7 48)9 49)10 50)12
51)12 52)12 53)12 54)3 55)3 56)11 57)12 58)5 59)3 60)3 61)2 62)8
63)3 64)3 65)5 66)9

Page 135

1) 69 2) 239 3) 11 4) 568 5) 29 6) 108 7) 72 8) 244 9) 72 10) 312 11)
160 12) 324 13) 380 14) 345 15) 78 16) 468 17) 210 18) 895

Page 137

1) 467 2) 285 3) 596 4) 478 5) 665 6) 356

Page 140

1) 266 2) 569 3) 346 4) 168 5) 189 6) 695

Page 141

1) 285 2) 474 3) 168 4) 388 5) 272 6) 568

Page 143

1)   34 2) 49 3) 29 4) 28 5) 25 6) 219 7) 116 8) 41 9) 416 10) 599 11) 143
12) 346 13) 177 14) 74 15) 49

Page 144

1) 23 2) 26 3) 109 4) 325 5) 174 6) 689 7) 378 8) 776 9) 558 10) 267 11) 168 12) 757 13) 383 14) 875

Page 145

1) 384 2) 568 3) 89 4) 478 5) 197 6) 699 7) 78 8) 778 9) 258 10) 86 11) 896 12) 148

Page 146

1) 2,906 2) 3,828 3) 5,482 4) 5,098 5) 1,705 6) 3,289 7) 2,772 8) 3,494 9) 7,273

Page 148

1) 3,657 2) 3,737 3) 4,028 4) 42 5) 457 6) 24 7) 1,421 8) 2,256 9) 2,179

Dr. Kathleen Fletcher Bacer is currently a professor and creator/
director of Azusa Pacific University's Online Master of Arts in Educational
Technology Program. Her expertise stems from 19 years of K-8 classroom
teaching and training teachers in classroom management and manipulative
math techniques. Daughter of a retired innovative science teacher and
mother of 3 daughters, her teaching models a belief that "critical to any
teaching/learning process is the ability to effectively connect with the learner
enabling them to construct a personal educational experience." As a
mathematics teacher nominee of the year (1984), Dodger Education Hero
Award (1991), Good Apple Award (1993), Teacher of the Year (1995-1996),
and in the Who's Who Among Americas Teachers (2004), she is known for
her innovative and creative techniques.

ISBN 1-41204126-0